The 30 Day Startup

Sam Kamani and William Schmidt

Contents

Introduction

With a great idea and a modest amount of cash, creating your own tech startup can be an extremely exciting and fulfilling endeavor. If you think of business as a sport, then tech startups are major league and funding support is rapidly growing.

In 2012, people couldn't fathom that the Instagram photo sharing app was acquired by Facebook for $1 billion. Then, in 2014, just two years later, Facebook acquired the messaging app WhatsApp for a mind blowing $19.3 billion.

Even if you're not interested in high profile billion dollar unicorns, thousands of under-the-radar software startups are quietly earning their founders and investors millions each year. With profit margins as high as 50%, the SaaS (software as a service) business model has created some of the most profitable businesses in history.

Unfortunately, starting a tech startup can also lead to significant losses, as well as a stressful professional and personal life at the beck and call of impatient investors

A much better way is to launch your startup with a Minimum Viable Product (MVP), one that can be shipped in six weeks or less. This will keep your bank account in the black, avoid high blood pressure, and maximise the chances of your tech startup succeeding (whatever your definition of success).

In the first part of this book, we take a look at how billion-dollar household names like Airbnb or Dropbox (as well as smaller not-so-famous but still successful and profitable startups) got off the ground by starting small, testing and iterating.

The next part covers growth strategies and practical tips, as well as case studies of startups that figured out ways to grow fast and profitably. Very rarely, especially these days, will a startup have access to millions of dollars of funding from day one, but for the purposes of this book we will assume you have a limited amount of capital at your disposal (we recommend a minimum of $30,000).

This isn't a book that needs to be read from cover to cover. Feel free to flip through to chapters that interest you most. We hope the following pages will inspire some brilliant new startups and nudge others off the starting block. Perhaps you?

Part 1:
Successful MVPs

What Multi-Billion Dollar Industry will be Created because of Your Startup?

There has never been a better time to be an entrepreneur. The digital revolution which spawned computers, transistors, microchips, programming languages – and later on, the Internet, personal computers and mobile devices – has created more opportunities to build world changing businesses than any other time in history.

Without any training in science, engineering or business, it is now possible for someone to invent a market disruptive product and, in so doing, create an entirely new industry out of thin air.

Swelling the ranks of multi-millionaires and billionaires worldwide, the tech startup ecosystem is the modern day equivalent of the gold rush. It is offering countless opportunities to create and innovate – whether by launching new websites, new apps, wearable devices or utilising the Internet of Things. And, as with any innovative breakthrough, new ecosystems of underlying businesses and professions spring to life.

> "The mobile device is now the television, and the television is now the radio."
>
> – Gary Vaynerchuk, Founder of VaynerMedia

To illustrate how this can happen, in 2010 Kevin Systrom and Mike Krieger launched Instagram – a photo sharing mobile app, which was a relatively simple idea in terms of innovation. Complex technologies such as Internet-connected mobile devices, digital cameras, mobile operating systems had, of course, already been invented. Instagram simply combined these technologies and created a mobile app using Apple's and Google's software development kit.

The simplicity of the app compared to Facebook caught on quickly with users. It had 100,000 downloads in the first week and 1 million users within two months. Of course, as the app's usage skyrocketed, what had begun as a simple app now required much more complex engineering to scale and handle the rapidly expanding user base. In the startup world, of course, that's a 'good problem' to have!

The company attracted more than $7 million of funding by early 2011. Then in April 2012, just 18 months after launching, it was acquired by Facebook for approximately $1 billion in cash and stock.

One billion dollars was a fantastic result for Instagram founders and early investors, but it doesn't begin to explain the value that the business continues to create. Entire new industries and professions owe their existence to Instagram.

Massive multi-million dollar creative agencies have been created out of Instagram, and the concept of "influencer marketing" has exploded. It has originated an entirely new career of 'Instagram Influencer', with such individuals now earning hundreds of thousands of dollars per year by promoting brands and holiday destinations – some can even earn upwards of $1 million for a single Instagram post.

And the ripples set in motion by Instagram are ever widening. Countless ecommerce stores have gone from zero to millions of dollars in annual sales from just one marketing strategy: paying Instagram influencers to promote their new product.

In New Zealand, a business school graduate Lyia Liu spent less than $10,000 creating an ecommerce website selling fabric waist trainers, which she ordered from China. Liu's sole marketing strategy has been marketing via Instagram and paying Instagram influencers to post photos of themselves wearing the product. Orders quickly came pouring in and, in under a year, her new business had made $3.5 million in sales, delivering almost $1 million in profits.

In the startup world, with unicorn startups and one billion dollar valuations, a $3–4 million company in New Zealand is small fry. But companies like Liu's wouldn't even exist if two young startup founders hadn't taken a punt in 2010 , and pressed ahead with their idea for a simpler, photo-focused social app.

Not every startup makes it to the front page of Forbes

Because the success stories are so impressive, more and more people are drawn to the startup world every day. But here a reality check is needed. Creating a new business, even just a brick and mortar shop, never guarantees success – and tech startups have even less guarantees.

According to Jessie Hagen of U.S. Bank, 82% of new businesses fail due to cash flow issues, and nearly 79% fail due to starting out with too little capital. However, big-time investment doesn't guarantee success.

Australian startup Guvera knows a thing or two about raising large sums of money and still floundering. Guvera started in 2008 as a music streaming company and managed to raise an eye watering $218 million in private funding. Yet the company lost $95 million in the 2015-2016 financial year with revenues of just $1.4 million.

Guvera was planning an Initial Public Offering (IPO) in 2017 but was blocked by the Australian Securities Exchange. Guvera's IPO prospectus was widely criticised and scrutiny from the Australian Securities and Investments Commission forced the company to issue an updated version with 45 amendments.

Another startup that reached unicorn status but failed is Mode Media. Known previously as Glam Media, Mode Media operated under the web properties of Glam.com, Brash.com, Bliss.com, Foodie.com, and Tend.com. At its peak, Mode Media was supposed to be worth more than a billion dollars and had thousands of content producers spread around the globe. In 2015, it generated more than $90 million of revenue. And in

2016, Mode Media was projected to exceed $100 million in revenue. However, the company folded in 2016.

Despite the large revenue figures, Mode hadn't become profitable and tried to evolve from a model making revenue from selling display adverts to one that encouraged crowdsourced video content and sold native adverts and video adverts inventory. None of these pivots worked, despite the quarter billion dollars that Mode Media had raised..

These are just a couple of cautionary stories to show that smart people with near limitless funding are not guaranteed to win the startup game, even when conventional business wisdom says they will.

At the same time, startups like Ring (formerly Doorbot) did prevail, despite a lack of early funding and most people ridiculing the concept.

When Jamie Siminoff went on ABC's 'Shark Tank' to pitch Doorbot in 2013, he believed his future hinged on getting an investment. His idea was very simple – a Wi-Fi enabled doorbell with a video camera to see who is outside the door. He wanted $700,000 for 10% of his company.

None of the judges were convinced. Only one, Kevin O'Leary, made an offer which Siminoff thought derisory. Having sunk in more than $10,000 of his own money, Siminoff left almost in tears.

But there was to be a significant silver lining: the free publicity his TV appearance generated. Ultimately Siminoff's product solved a real problem and the orders starting coming in. The rest is history; in February 2018, Amazon acquired Ring for $1 billion.

Start with a Minimum Viable Product

If it's not lack of funding, what is the key differentiator between startups that succeed, and the majority that fail?

In The Lean Startup (2011), Eric Ries argues that the main reason startups fail is because they spend far too long trying to build the perfect product only to launch, almost out of money, with a "perfect" product... that nobody wants.

Historically, this approach to launching a product has worked well for existing markets with years of data to make decisions. But for startups, where a market may not even exist, targeting success via traditional means is akin to trying to win the lottery.

A great business idea isn't enough. You need to quickly and cheaply test your assumptions to establish whether your product meets the needs of a market and fills this niche well enough for people to pay for it.

The early days of a startup should involve constraint testing, tweaking and learning with the ultimate goal of discovering product/market fit. Your product should solve a painful problem and be something the market both needs and wants. Once you have met this criteria, you can double down on improving and refining the product, raising funding and shooting for the stars.

Start small and embrace failure

Sometimes it is only fear of failure that stops would-be entrepreneurs from pursuing their startup ideas. Even if they don't care about losing money or wasting months in development, they hate the idea of creating a business and then seeing it flounder.

This is where a Minimum Viable Product (MVP) offers an invaluable safety net. An MVP is created when you build a very basic version of your product to enable you to test your assumptions as cheaply and quickly as possible. If the MVP is successful and sparks enthusiastic feedback, you can persevere and look to build a fuller version of your product.

If your MVP launches to deafening silence, you have the opportunity to rethink or pivot on the idea. After all, you've successfully tested out your hypothesis. Now you can go back to the drawing board and adjust accordingly.

> "An MVP is a process that you repeat over and over again: identify your riskiest assumption, find the smallest possible experiment to test that assumption, and use the results of the experiment to course correct."
>
> – Yevgeniy Brikman, Co-founder of Gruntwork

Although an MVP is often a functional working product, it can be even simpler than that. It could be a clickable prototype that you show to relevant people in the industry; it could be a YouTube video of the problem and the potential solution you hope to build; or it could involve selling a manual service (to be later automated with software once the idea has been validated by people paying for it).

The overarching goal of an MVP is to test whether there is enough demand to justify spending time and money on building the full version of the product. The test can be as simple as charging people to use your MVP – if people are happy to pay for the MVP version, they will be even happier with your full version.

Sometimes your MVP will be too basic to warrant charging money, or it won't actually be a usable product. If that's the case, there are other ways to measure demand and judge whether your MVP has been a success:

- Asking for pre-signups (offering a special deal to sign up before the full product launches).

- Asking for email-signups so users can stay in the loop as the full product is built.

- Monitoring usage and other user behaviour of your MVP (which could be a static website) using tools such as Google Analytics.

- Offering a 'Pro' version with pricing options, but informing users it is 'currently in development' when anyone clicks on it for more information.

By starting with an MVP, you don't need to fear failure. You're not putting millions of dollars or a year of development on the line. All you're doing is testing your ideas and being prepared to start with something unpolished.

"It's critical to understand that an MVP is not the product with fewer features. Rather it is the simplest thing that you can show to customers to get the most learning at that point in time."

– Steve Blank, Founder of multiple startups

The concept of building MVPs is not something reserved for startups. It's now a common tactic used by large corporates looking to stay innovative, such as Microsoft and Google.

"In big companies...many months are spent on planning features and arguing details with the goal of everyone reaching an agreement on what is the 'right' thing for the customer. That may be the right approach for shrink-wrapped software, but with the web we have an incredible advantage. Just ship it! Let the user tell you if it's the right thing and if it's not. Hey you can fix it and ship it to the web the same day if you want!"

– Sanaz Ahari, Program Manager at Microsoft

Your MVP should take weeks to make, not months

Having a fantastic idea for a new business is like falling in love. The idea is constantly on your mind, and even the most mundane activities end up being enjoyable as you run through the idea over and over in your mind.

At this point, it's tempting to jump all in. Having visualised the dream product, you want to start building it right away. While this passion is great, and is the way many startups begin, it's only going to take you so far. And if you never achieve product/market fit, your enthusiasm will wane as you struggle to make your business profitable.

The answer is to test the waters with an MVP. Take your product idea and shave it down until it is just one dedicated tool that you can build in a few weeks – a tool that solves a specific problem. Build just that product, promote it, and gather feedback. Then you'll have real data to decide on your next course of action.

This is the same path that billion dollar startups like Dropbox, Airbnb, and Zappos took. It's also the path that countless smaller startups have headed down and by doing so are now making millions of dollars without having to raise equity or debt.

The founders of these startups all had big ideas. Some ideas were so big they required years of development, yet they were all able to ship an initial MVP in a matter of weeks, sometimes days, and in some cases less than one day.

The ability to cull your idea down and ship an MVP fast is a huge indicator of how successful your Startup will be.

- How could you build an MVP version of your product it in a matter of days or weeks, not months?

- What is the core functionality you could focus on while ignoring every other possible feature?

The following chapters focus on how successful startups built the first MVP version of their ideas. Some of the MVPs were actual usable products, others were creative ways to test the concept and gauge whether the business model was worth pursuing.

Baremetrics: A Million Dollar Analytics Startup that took Seven days to Build

Startup: Baremetrics

Product: Analytics dashboard

Time to build MVP: Seven days (spread across a month)

Started: November 2013

Current annual run rate: $1.2m

Current employees: Eight

Josh Pigford is a serial entrepreneur who was already working on two startups when he had an idea for building an analytics dashboard. It was a 'scratch your own itch' idea – he looked for the ideal solution and couldn't find it.

Both of his businesses used Stripe to process payments, so he wanted to track the data from Stripe and present it in easy-to-read metrics to track progress of important KPIs such as MRR (monthly recurring revenue), LTV (lifetime value), monthly churn and ARR (annual run rate).

Business dashboards weren't a new concept at the time – Geckoboard had launched back in 2010 with $1.8 million in funding. But Josh was searching for a simple solution that just focused on the few metrics that mattered to a SaaS startup.

As he was already working on two businesses, Josh couldn't spend months building a polished product. Instead, he worked around his schedule and managed to build a basic first version of the product in just seven working days over the course of a month.

His launch marketing strategy was even simpler. He sent out some tweets on Twitter, which is how he got his first 10 paying customers.

> *"That first version was raw. It didn't do anywhere close to everything I felt like it really needed to do. There were a lot of manual processes that wouldn't scale. The design was rough around the edges. But you know what? It didn't matter. That first incomplete, unscalable version got me to $2,000 in monthly recurring revenue in around eight weeks."*
>
> - Josh Pigford, Founder of Baremetrics

Launch early and make it a paid product.

Josh charged for the product from day one because he wanted early proof that it was a product idea worth pursuing. And after the product was live, it was much more valuable to get feedback from real paying customers about what features to develop next than listen to people trying it out for free.

> *"Reduce the timeframe between building software and it being used by paying customers, and the speed at which you can grow your business will increase exponentially."*
>
> - Josh Pigford, Founder of Baremetrics

Josh continued working on multiple businesses for the first few months that Baremetrics was running. However, it soon made sense to exit both of the other businesses and with his sole focus on the new product, he was able to grow it into a fully fledged business and raise $800k in seed funding. The company now has an annual run rate of $1.2 million with a team of eight people.

Growing the business wasn't without its struggles though. During the early stage growth of the company, copycat competitors were emerging almost every week.

Rather than worrying about these new competitors, Josh kept his focus on making Baremetrics better and after a few years the company branched out to offer multiple payment providers (including Braintree Payments and Recurly) along with an API, which allows customers to pull in data from other external sources, as well as their own internal data sources.

Another interesting way Baremetrics has gained traction is by spearheading the 'Open Startups' approach to transparency. This allows customers to make their dashboards public and Baremetics led the way by making its own dashboard accessible to all. Anyone can go to the Baremetrics website and find out how many customers the company has, what its churn rate is and how much revenue it makes each month.

Other notable multi-million dollar startups have since opted to make their Baremetrics dashboards 'open', such as Buffer, ConvertKit, Hubstaff and launch27. This unique approach gains media exposure for these startups, but a side benefit for Baremetrics is that it always results in traffic coming to the Baremetrics website.

Egghead.io: From Free YouTube Screencasts to a $3m Startup

Startup: egghead.io

Product: Online education streaming service

Time to build MVP: Two weeks

Started: November 2013

Current annual run rate: $3.3m

Current employees: 12

Joel Hooks knew he wanted to achieve financial independence and decided the means to do that was to start a business. His first attempt at this was building a software product for semi-professional photographers, but he quickly realised this was never going to be a good fit for his existing skills and networks.

Searching for a more viable alternative, he identified an opportunity to meet a growing demand for learning AngularJS (a JavaScript programming framework). Initially, he planned to write an ebook and sell it online, but soon realised he could shortcut this process, as well as provide more value.

A friend of his, John Lindquist, was already making free screencasts teaching AngularJS on YouTube. As John's videos were getting lots of views and comments, Joel casually pitched an idea to him – why not package these screenshots as a product and sell them outside of YouTube?

At first, John decided to just stick with uploading his videos to YouTube (the company had indicated he could soon start earning from the videos), but Joel was persistent and eventually persuaded him to join as a co-founder.

The first version of egghead.io took just two weeks. John compressed 50 of his video screencasts into a single zip file and sent them to Joel who created what was essentially a blog with embedded videos for blog posts. The videos were hosted on Wistia, which meant only basic server requirements, and the blog posts were hidden from public view until a user subscribed via Stripe (a third party payment gateway).

The co-founders had a very basic marketing launch strategy. John had an existing email subscriber list, so he simply sent out an email containing a link to the MVP product. As a result, egghead.io got its first paying customers and earned $6,500 in sales the first week from one-off $50 purchases.

After this initial validation of their MVP, Joel and John decided to switch to a subscription model. Despite having no additional videos in their library (just the initial 50 screencasts they launched with), they decided to pitch the offer of a $99 per year subscription to get access to premium screencasts every month.

Another early win ensued – a second promotional email to the same list resulted in multiple signups to the $99 offer. However, this created an urgent problem. Egghead.io needed to quickly find more video instructors (it couldn't rely on John to produce new content every week). And of course, not just any instructors;

with YouTube as an alternative source of free content, quality was more important than quantity.

At first, the co-founders looked to their immediate network of friends and when that pool of talent ran dry, they had to reach out to cold prospects. N.B growing and maintaining a two-sided marketplace is always a tricky problem to solve (you need enough subscribers to pay the bills, but you need enough highly skilled content producers to maintain the library and keep subscribers around).

Joel and John quickly realised that happy and effective instructors result in a more exciting content library, which in turn makes it easier to capture new subscribers (and retain existing ones). Over the the past five years, they've built up a thriving community of egghead.io instructors and created different ways of helping and serving them (including creating dedicated separate websites such as howtoegghead.com.

> "The most significant mistake I see [startup entrepreneurs] make is that they start with the solution. They think they see a problem, and they jump straight to the idea. Then they build the idea before they have any customers."

> – Joel Hooks, Founder of egghead.io

Having been profitable since it launched, egghead.io has opted not to raise venture capital, and has grown steadily. The company now has a team of 12 employees and the website brings in $270,000 in monthly recurring revenue.

iDoneThis: Lawyer makes a Productivity App with over 160,000 Users

Startup: iDoneThis

Product: Team productivity tracking, software-as-a-service

Time to build MVP: Two weeks

Started: January 2011

Current annual run rate: $7.6m (estimated)

Current employees: 10 (estimated)

The 'mobile first' approach to building a startup is fairly common. It was famously the approach used by Mark Zuckerberg in the early stages of building Facebook when he recognised that mobiles would one day be the primary way users would interact with his product.

Unfortunately taking a mobile first approach won't usually mean a quicker-to-market MVP. That's because designing and building a native mobile app, or even a progressive web app, can take a lot of time.

When Walter Chen and Rodrigo Guzman decided to build iDoneThis, they decided to build an 'email first' product after considering 'web first' and 'mobile first' options. The 'email first' approach meant they were able to finish their MVP in less than two weeks, drastically cutting down time to market their product.

Walter Chen actually started his career as a lawyer but, frustrated with his job, he caught the startup bug and moved to San Francisco where he conceived the idea for iDoneThis. The concept combined Jerry Seinfeld's 'don't break the chain' productivity technique with peer accountability for consistently doing tasks each day. The product was very simple – once signed up, customers would receive one email per day, and they could simply hit reply and start typing their updates for that day. Without requiring users to log into a website, the iDoneThis server would receive the email reply, transcode it, and collate it into a digest so that productivity and accomplishments were tracked.

Initially, the product was given away for free. Users would enter their email address, similar to signing up to an email newsletter, and the next day they would receive a first email asking them what they had accomplished that day.

Due to the speed of MVP build, iDoneThis was able to launch right at the beginning of January when people were making New Year's resolutions. The startup managed to get 200 signups in the first week by casually promoting its website on various Internet forums.

Users would sign up for a variety of reasons: from tracking their work accomplishments to building a productivity habit, or even to quit smoking.

Signups gradually increased, but it wasn't until April 2011 – when the product was picked up and showcased on Lifehacker – that its user base increased from hundreds to thousands.

After the Lifehacker article, Chen and Guzman decided there was enough traction to double down on the business. They joined the startup incubator AngelPad and shifted the positioning of the product to focus on funded startups and corporates, while no longer offering free accounts.

Managers were able to sign up and add all the members of their team as users. After the daily email was sent asking users to list their accomplishments that day, responses were collated and sent out to the entire team so that everyone could see what others had contributed.

Without too many significant changes to their initial MVP, Chen and Guzman were able to find their product/market fit. From there, marketing and promotion became easier because they could focus their efforts on more lucrative customers (as opposed to the more general habit or self-improvement crowds). Revenue per customer increased, user churn decreased, and converting users to a paid account was an easier sell as the cost was a comparatively low business expense for most customers.

Too simple to succeed?

Ever since its launch, iDoneThis attracted lots of criticism, particularly from other tech startups and software engineers who couldn't believe people would pay money each month to use a tool they could "write themselves in a weekend". Whether those naysayers went on to actually build their own tool or not, the product continued to grow. Despite its simplicity (or maybe because of it), iDoneThis solved a problem that business owners and managers need solving – keeping track of a growing team and making sure everyone is staying productive.

This simple "email first" startup went on to raise $900,000 in seed funding. By sticking with a narrow product focus and heavily investing in content marketing, the founders continued to grow the business which currently has 160,000 users and a customer base which includes well known companies such as Zappos, Shopify, Mozilla and Tripadvisor.

After running the startup for five years, Chen and Guzman eventually sold the business in 2016.

Followup Edge: A Functional MVP Built in three weeks with No Coding

Startup: Followup Edge

Product: Lead follow-up automation service

Time to build MVP: Three weeks

Started: January 2018

Current annual run rate: $420,000

Current employees: Three

You can't build a SaaS platform without hiring an expensive software engineer, right? Wrong. Scottie Schneider built the first MVP for his startup Followup Edge without writing a single line of code!

Making sure you contact sales leads as quickly as possible (ideally before your competitor does) is a well known rule of service businesses. Schneider and his co-founders were running an ad agency and were having issues when some of their clients blamed them for getting 'bad leads'. Investigating the matter, it soon became clear that these clients had sloppy follow up processes.

The founders tried to figure out a solution that would automate the follow-up process and ensure clients could start talking to their leads directly as quickly as possible. They looked at existing tools such as Active Campaign, but quickly realised they would need to build something more customised due to the need to make follow-up communication look as genuine and spam-free as possible.

The prototype would need to take inbound leads through an automated sequence of SMS messages, emails, and direct voicemails that stopped as soon as a lead responded. If the messages continued to send after the conversation had started, that would spell disaster!

Scottie Schneider had experience in fullstack web development, but he knew it would take him far too long to build something from scratch. The team meanwhile didn't want to spend money on a software engineer without validating the product idea first.

Scottie ended up using Bubble (a drag-and-drop web tool editor) and integrating with Zapier (a visual API integration tool) to build a fully functional MVP in just three weeks. He was able to achieve such a short build time because he didn't have to write a single line of code, nor did he have any server requirements – that was all handled by Bubble.

By spreading the word with existing clients, the MVP was bringing in revenue two weeks after launch. Then the company targeted other ad agencies already in their professional network, promising them better conversion rates for their clients.

Shortly after launching, Followup Edge set up a referral reward program in which a share of profit per customer was given back to the ad agency that referred them. This referral scheme has been the company's sole form of marketing to date and the main way it is expanding its customer base.

> "You could say we've grown through affiliate marketing, but at the end of the day it's really just understanding who we're actually serving: the ad agency. We make their life easier, and in return they get as many of their clients as they can on the platform. It's a beautifully symbiotic relationship."

> – Scottie Schneider, Founder of Followup Edge

Expanding tech stack only as needed

The startups's initial, very minimal tech stack of Bubble and Zapier has evolved as the operation has grown. Although the company eventually needed some timing critical functionality to run separately on a Node.js server, it has kept the rest of the front end running on Bubble.

Now that the idea for Followup Edge has been validated and its revenue is growing each month, the company's long term plans will eventually involve replacing Bubble with a fully customised web application written from scratch.

> "Build first, then worry about scalability. You simply can't anticipate every problem that 10 customers will bring, much less 100."

> – Scottie Schneider, Founder of Followup Edge

What if you don't have the money or skills to build a functioning MVP?

If they don't have the skills or money, many people assume the only way to build a product is to raise seed funding in order to get the runway to design and build the software.

Unfortunately, what many early-stage entrepreneurs fail to realise is that getting access to that kind of capital is not an easy task. Gone are the days when you could get your first million by having a .com domain, a nice logo and a slick PowerPoint presentation.

Ideas are a dime a dozen. There are thousands of people who will swear they had the idea for Uber several years before the company started. What is valuable in today's world is clever and effective execution of ideas. It was Uber that actually went out and created the network of drivers and demand from users.

Investors might be happy to listen to your idea, but unless you can show them some traction, they won't be investing $1 in you, let alone $1 million.

But how do you get traction for your product if you don't have the money or skills to make it?

Maybe your product idea is ginormous and has to be perfect to work (AI for the medical industry)? Or maybe it is a simple solution, but you're not a designer or programmer?

If this is your situation, there are three viable routes for you to take which have been used by successful startups (such as Dropbox, Tuft & Needle, and Zappos) to validate their business ideas and markets.

1. Landing Page MVP (Dropbox style)

If you have a great idea, but can't yet build the product, one of the best first steps is to build a Dropbox style MVP, i.e a one page website that includes a video and an email opt-in form.

In the case of Dropbox, Drew Houston had already built a prototype of the software, but this was not a necessary component. Just create some mockups of your software idea using design software or even something as simple as Keynote or PowerPoint. Once you've designed a few screens, create hotspots on buttons pointing to the different screens.

What you'll have now is a non-functional clickable prototype. It doesn't need to have pixel perfect design – just explain it's an early alpha version and is currently in development.

The next step is to create a screencast of the software being used, either by recording your computer screen as you click through various parts of your design; or, alternatively, you can load the prototype on your smartphone and record your thumb tapping through various screens.

If you've got some basic video editing skills, you can create this in a day. Or if you decide you need extra polish, you can hire a freelancer or design agency to make something more professional (you'll still be paying far less than you would for building a functional piece of software).

And remember, as you're showcasing this in a video, you don't need to design every screen of your app, just the few screens you need to demonstrate the value your product will provide.

Once you have the video, you can create a simple one page website, showcasing your product idea, and including an email opt-in form to capture email addresses of interested users.

The final step is marketing your website: getting the link in front of as many relevant people as possible. Email your network, promote it to your friends on Facebook and followers on Twitter. If necessary, you can run a short campaign on Facebook or Google Ads.

TIP: Give an option on the email opt-in form that allows you to contact some users. Not every user will check this, but for those that do, you can ask them questions and dig deeper into the problem you're solving and the possible use cases.

Your website may not go viral like the Dropbox video did, but as you promote it and gather more email addresses, you'll be able to have conversations with more potential users.

From here you can take your findings and decide on the next step. Perhaps this will be fleshing out the clickable prototype and arranging some one-to-one demos with some of the people you've been speaking with. Or maybe the response was compelling enough to go to a startup incubator or seed accelerator and present a case for early stage seed funding.

2. The Concierge MVP

While the Landing Page MVP is an effective way to build buzz and anticipation, it doesn't fully validate the economics behind your startup idea. Will people actually pay you money? Will users subscribe on a monthly basis?

Investors will always be impressed if you can show your startup already has paying users, but if your concept is too technologically complex to build with limited resources, what can you do?

The answer is selling your product as a concierge service rather than as an app or web application. You can create a website, even a mobile app if you need, but when people sign up the service is actually achieved via humans rather than software.

Maybe you've got an idea for an AI powered online dating app. Instead of spending months building a rudimentary prototype, you could start with a website asking people to fill out a questionnaire, telling them you'll be in touch soon with potential matches.

Or perhaps you want to build a real estate tool with a complex algorithm that matches home buyers with the perfect house based on their location, work location, school requirements and lifestyles. This would take months to build something even marginally usable. However, a concierge model could be achieved in one day by simply processing each request offline with the help of some smart researchers and a knowledgeable real estate agent.

Neither of these examples would scale when you have thousands of new users each day. But that doesn't matter, because before you get to that problem, you'll have validated the market for your new product idea. Will people use it? Will people pay to use it?

In some cases, you can build initial cash flow for your startup via concierge services, and then use this to self-fund developing the software solution which will eventually replace it.

3. The Wizard of Oz MVP

You can take a concierge-backed MVP to the next level by making it a 'Wizard of Oz' MVP. This is when you build a website and/or an app which (as far as the user can tell) works like any other piece of software. Users can log in, complete requests or orders and get the result they're after.

On the backend, though, instead of a complicated algorithm or advanced AI, the majority of effort (or sometimes all of it) is handled by humans. The fact that it's not a fully software solution can be obfuscated by showing users a processing screen and notifying them later with an email or push notification to show the result.

Let's say you want to build an app that connects professional security guards and allows you to hire them privately for a one-off job or for ongoing work (for example, while you're having a large party, or perhaps following an incident of theft).

Creating an Uber-styled app that programmatically handles all of this would be a complex task. Instead, you could create a shell for the app which acts as a glorified contact form. Once submitted, humans would handle the process of locating an available security guard and organising the job, handling the payment to the security guard and confirming all the details with you.

Users of the app would have no idea that everything was happening by human effort and, more importantly, they wouldn't care. They would be getting the end result they were after when they downloaded the app.

Besides validating the business idea, the advantage of starting with a Wizard of Oz type app is that you can slowly improve your processes and incrementally replace various human tasks with software. For example, instead of phoning a list of possible security guards, you could build a small application that allows the human operator to choose likely security guards. Then the software would handle sending them an SMS and programmatically accept the first one who responds.

Later on you could extend this, so the list of security guards is programmatically selected, based on available schedules for individual security guards and the locations for which they are available.

The Hybrid Software Startup

Analysts tell us that Uber, one of the most successful software startups in recent years and currently valued at $76 billion, will never become fully profitable until all of its fleet is made up of self-driving vehicles.

Even today, the company is losing money on every passenger booking a ride with Uber and is making up the difference through investor funding. Uber's founders will have already crunched the numbers when they started the company, but they went ahead anyway. Like Jeff Bezos who grew Amazon by negative profits for twenty straight years, they are in it for the long game.

Their goal and vision is for Uber to become the world's ubiquitous travel company. To achieve that goal, they essentially built an app as a concierge MVP. Instead of self-driving cars, they'd got an army of human drivers taking up the role of self-driving cars.

The human drivers will gradually be replaced, In the meantime, Uber is in the twenty year phase that Amazon was in. The company is growing its market share, albeit unprofitably, so that when 100% self driving cars are a reality, it will have the user base to seamlessly service a massive user base and finally return a profit for their investors.

Perhaps you have an idea for a software startup that is so wild, the smartest engineers are telling you it's not possible. They might be telling the truth for now, but that doesn't mean you can't start the company. Take a page from Uber's startup book: launch by using software for the parts that can be achieved programmatically and, for everything else, use human labour.

Set your MVP budget and choose your pathway

Whatever budget you have to work with, don't use it as an excuse to hold off on building your MVP. Some of the techniques we've written about can be implemented very cheaply for your first version.

Please note that this section is written with a non-technical founder in mind.

Up to $1,000 or "I just want to test the idea and see whether it'll float"

With $1,000 or less to invest, a Landing Page MVP is probably the go-to option. Present the problem you're solving and describe the product idea.

Another option is to create a Concierge MVP – create a landing page and embed a Typeform form (www.typeform.com). This means when customers submit an enquiry, you can fulfil the service manually yourself (or use a third party).

It is also worth checking out marketplaces like 1KProjects.com or SideProjectors.com. There may be a website someone else has made that can easily be adapted for your market.

Once you've got a landing page or website, a guerilla marketing approach will be needed. Rather than spending money on ads, reach out to your network and ask for favors to share the website URL to get wider reach.

Up to $5,000 or "I'm fairly confident in the idea, but want to test if it's something people will actually use"

This size of budget should allow you to develop a Concierge MVP by using a combination of tools such as Bubble (www.bubble.is) or Typeform. There should be enough in the kitty to customize the look and feel of your website, as well as pay a freelancer to sort out technical issues you can't fix.

Alternatively, you could stick with a Landing Page MVP and use the budget to pay a freelance UX Designer to design some screens of your proposed product to display as images or a video.

Ideally, you should leave around half of your budget to spend on marketing. This will allow you to get the website in front of your model customers via demographic targeting on Facebook or Google Ads.

Up to $30,000 or "I have some initial paying customers who will use it"

At this level, you should be able to build a fully functional prototype of your product idea as long as it is ultra focused and solves just one major problem. Your budget should allow for paying a freelance full-stack developer to build a custom web application, but it is vital to guard against scope creep. By adding in just one additional feature, you could introduce unforeseen technical complexity, which will blow your development budget.

Allow around $10,000 in this budget for marketing and promoting the prototype. Consider guest posting and paying influencers to get a wider reach in your market.

Up to $50,000 or "I'm already confident in the idea and want to prove the concept and take it to potential investors"

With this sort of budget, you can build a fully functional MVP using a freelancer or development shop. Although agencies will be more expensive, they are less risky because all the technical knowledge won't be confined in one freelancer's head.

Remember, you still need to limit your development costs to leave room for marketing. With this budget, we'd recommend leaving $15,000–$20,000 to spend on marketing.

Dropbox: $10B Company was Validated with an MVP Built in Less than a Day

Startup: Dropbox

Product: File hosting and backup service

Time to build MVP: One day (non-functional)

Started: May 2007

Current annual run rate: $1.4b

Current employees: 1,858 (estimated)

Back in the early 2000s, the de facto way to share and access files between different friends and users was through thumb drives and email. This caused issues if you had a large file, or if you forgot your thumbdrive, or you simply wanted access to a file on your computer but had no way to get it.

Drew Houston was travelling on a bus from Boston to New York when he'd forgotten his thumb drive which had crucial files he needed for the trip. This was extremely frustrating for him, not least because it wasn't the first time he'd made the mistake. He literally opened his laptop, while on the bus, and started writing code to create a digital solution to this problem.

He wanted a world where, no matter what computer or device you were working on, you'd have access to all your important data.

How to create an MVP when your product is solving a big problem?

A lot of startups can be created by building a simple first version in a few weeks, throwing it out in the wild, getting feedback and then iterating. The problem with Dropbox was not that an MVP would be difficult or expensive to make, but rather that it needed to work 100 times out of 100, if people were to switch to it as a way to store, access and share their files.

Dropbox was going to have to integrate with the computer's operating system, handle file synchronisation, file conflicts, and test thousands of edge cases to ensure the software didn't inadvertently delete someone's important data. Making a first version of software that worked that well was going to require significant time and money.

> "While you want to launch fast and iterate, people don't like that if you're doing that with their wedding photos or their tax returns."

> - Drew Houston, Founder of Dropbox

Instead of spending months programming, Drew decided to get exposure for his product idea by creating a video demonstrating the problem Dropbox solved and how the solution would work. He created a landing page with the video embedded, and put an email sign up form under the video, so that people could join his waiting list to get beta access to the software.

This wasn't agency quality video production. Just a voice-over screencast of Houston's computer as he demonstrated the problem that Dropbox solved and how simple the product would be.

The video, which Houston created late one evening, essentially became a non-functional MVP to gauge whether the product was going to solve a big enough problem. After posting a link to the website online, the video drew hundreds of thousands of views and 70,000 people added their email to his waiting list.

Drew used this early validation to apply to the Y Combinator startup accelerator and find a co-founder, Arash Ferdowsi, to help him build the software. Together, they continued building the functional product and were able to secure $1.2 million in seed funding through the Y-Combinator demo day.

With initial funding in place, they could obtain the talent and resources they needed to build the first official version of Dropbox (which didn't publicly launch until September 2008).

Making Dropbox go viral

Dropbox continued to utilise content marketing (video demonstrations) to build buzz and market their product, but switched to a different strategy after its launch – an incentive referral program. If you invited a friend to use Dropbox, both you and your friend would receive free extra storage space.

Many people loved the simplicity of Dropbox and the extra incentive to share turned some users into evangelists for the product. The free accounts allowed 2GB of space (which was very generous at the time), but users were able to increase their free storage space to 20GB or more. Some even set up their own online advertising campaigns paying AdWords to get users to sign up – it's an impressive feat to get your own customers to pay money to advertise your own product for you!

Just a feature, not a product?

From early on Dropbox had plenty of critics, particularly those in the tech space. They claimed it was an unnecessary product because people could simply get an FTP account and synchronise this to a folder on multiple computers.

What these people failed to realise, and what Houston was able to validate with his initial MVP (the landing page video), was that most people using a computer are not technical enough to set this up. A done-for-you solution that just works was the main attraction to the product.

As Dropbox grew to hundreds of thousands of users, the company caught the notice of Steve Jobs who invited Houston to a meeting and briefly discussed a possible acquisition. The founders, however, wanted to remain an independent company, which led Jobs to warn them that Dropbox was essentially a feature, not a product and that Apple could easily build their own version making Dropbox superfluous.

> "A lot of the problems that he cited were not really specific to Dropbox so, while it's true that we're not going to make Dropbox work better than what became iCloud on an iPhone, Apple has the same issue if they want iCloud to work seamlessly on

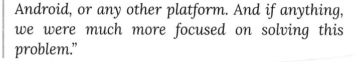

Android, or any other platform. And if anything, we were much more focused on solving this problem."

– Drew Houston, Founder of Dropbox

Houston acknowledged the potential issues (they were never going to be able to integrate with MacOS or Windows as closely as the Apple or Microsoft could), but he also knew that the reason Dropbox was so successful was because they were able to build a narrow product that solved a specific problem better than any other product. People now had access to all their important files, on any device or operating system, and a simple way to share their files with anyone who needed them.

The narrow focus has paid off. The company eventually went public, and now has over 500 million users and over 12 million paying customers.

Buffer: From an Idea to Paying Customers in 7 weeks

Startup: Buffer

Product: Social media management tool, software-as-a-service

Time to build MVP: Seven weeks (over nights & weekends) + one week of validation

Started: November 2010

Current annual run rate: $18.6m

Current employees: 70

While Joel Gascoigne was trying to build and promote his startup OnePage (a startup for online business cards which failed to gain enough traction) he discovered that the more he contributed and shared content on Twitter, the more followers and engagement he got. This was the seed to his idea of automating the process to save time while further increasing engagement with his audience on social media.

Surely if he built a tool which saved him time, and provided him tangible benefits, it would be a product others would pay for as well? However, instead of jumping in and starting the project, he wanted to learn from some of his earlier mistakes and opted to take a much more "leaner" approach to launching this new app idea.

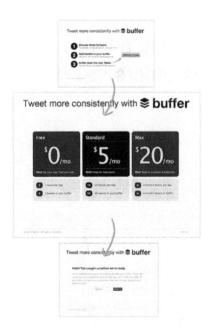

In fact, arguably the first MVP for Buffer wasn't even a working app, but rather a landing page with a link to a fake pricing page! Before any code was written, Joel wanted to check he wasn't going to end up building a product that didn't fix a big enough pain point.

He promoted the link to his two page website and tracked the number of people that clicked through to the pricing page and selected a plan (users were then informed the product wasn't ready yet).

Based on activity, email conversations and overall buzz around the website, Joel decided to take it to the next step and build a functioning product.

When it came to building the first version of the working product, there was a strong temptation to build a tool that supported both of the leading social networks used for sharing content at the time – Twitter and Facebook. Learning from his previous startup, Joel resisted this temptation and decided to cut the initial version of Buffer down to just handle sharing of content on Twitter (the pain point which he felt resonated with most people).

> "...it was wise to start with only Twitter since we wanted to make a product which was great at just a few things, rather than 'just ok' at many."
>
> – Joel Gascoigne, Founder of Buffer

The first version of Buffer was "finished" in seven weeks time, working just weekends and nights. In Joel's mind, the product was nowhere near finished and was still missing vital features, but he'd committed to a specific launch date and decided to push it live at the end of November 2010.

Joel promoted the web app on Twitter and Hacker News and immediately got around 100 users trying it out and had his first paying customer within four days of launching. After a month, he had three paying customers which gave him the confidence to double down on his efforts and continue adding functionality while also marketing it wider across the Internet.

Despite the quick-to-market MVP approach, Buffer still wasn't an overnight success. It took about six months until revenue from the product was enough for Joel to quit his day job (freelance web development). He then had to bring in a co-founder to help manage the community and drive content marketing. Subsequently, revenues grew further which triggered the company's move from the UK to take advantage of San Francisco's local startup ecosystem.

Buffer eventually caught the eyes of VC investors and was able to raise $450,000 in seed funding; and later in 2014, it raised a further $3.5 million in a Series A round of capital which gave the company a $60 million valuation.

By taking a lean approach and being profitable from the get-go, Buffer was able to grow on its own terms. The company gave up only 6.2% without giving any investor board seats. Since that time it has become even more profitable and, in July 2018, Buffer made the decision to buy out its main Series A investors for $3.3m using cash in its business bank account.

> "The advice I always give [to help early stage founders] is to try and cut as much as possible out of the first version of the product. That way, when you launch, you'll hopefully have fairly binary feedback: either people love that one feature, or they don't find it useful. It's easier to figure out what to build out from a single feature people love, than to launch with a bunch of things and figure out what is working and what isn't."
>
> – Joel Gascoigne, Founder of Buffer

Airbnb: How Fewer than 5 Users Validated Starting a $30b Company

Startup: Airbnb

Product: P2P Accommodation marketplace

Time to build MVP: 2-3 days

Started: October 2007

Current annual run rate: $2.6b

Current employees: 4,000 (estimated)

Today, Airbnb is a darling of the VC startup world, valued at over $30 billion. Back in late 2007, though, the idea began with a couple of roommates who needed extra income to cover rent.

Brian Chesky and Joe Gebbia, a couple of designers living in the very expensive San Francisco area, briefly considered simply adding a posting to Craigslist. Instead, they decided to register a domain name and have a bit of fun making a standalone website to solve their problem.

Not wanting to buy any extra furniture, the only kind of beds they could offer were airbeds. They called the website 'Airbed & Breakfast' and created a simple website with a few details about the accommodation, the price and a map.

This initial, ultra light MVP was not a two-way marketplace. It was simply a way for Chesky and Gebbia to advertise barebones accommodation at their own place while a conference was running in the city. It managed to attract three customers, each paying $80.

Apart from extra lunch money, the MVP gave validation to the idea that people could be willing to pay money to stay at a stranger's house, rather than renting traditional accommodation.

This insight led the pair to team up with Nathan Blecharczyk, a programmer and former roommate, who helped them validate the other side of that equation. Would people list a bed in their own homes for a stranger to book?

Still under the name Airbed & Breakfast, the second version of MVP took a lot longer to build, but the startup was still able to launch the new version of its website to coincide with the 2008 SXSW conference in San Francisco.

That's when Airbnb was truly born and the rest is history? Not exactly. The promotion during SXSW didn't come close to shattering anyone's expectations – it generated a grand total of two bookings for that month.

When you look under the surface, there are hardly any 'overnight successes' in life, and the founders decided that at least some validation – from both sides of the marketplace – was better than no validation at all.

The founders applied to join Y Combinator, a startup accelerator, and kept growing the website –but decided to focus on specific cities at a time, starting with

Denver. This allowed them to control the quality of their listings and was a similar approach to the one used by Facebook for its initial launch (allowing only specific universities at a time).

Growth-hacking their user base

With a working MVP, and early validation that the marketplace concept might work, Airbnb needed to quickly expand its database of rooms and accommodation. No one was going to care about the website if it only had a few dozen places to stay.

At the time, Craigslist was a key place to look for accommodation if you weren't going to stay at a traditional hotel or motel. The founders knew the existing accommodation listings on Craigslist would perform much better on a dedicated website that they'd designed. But how could they get these people onto their own website?

They ended up creating their own script which would mine Craigslist and get contact information for all its accommodation listings, which would then allow room owners to be contacted and pitched to list on Airbnb instead.

Some may argue this approach was below the belt, but there's no denying that anyone building a market disrupting product is going to poach existing customers off other competitors, the Airbnb founders simply found a way to automate the process.

Improving quality

A key turning point for Airbnb was when it hired a professional grade camera to take accommodation photographs of its listings in the New York area.

Until then, most of their accommodation listings were very amateurish, mainly due to poorly taken photos (at a time when smartphone cameras were still more of a gimmick than an actual utility). The change to professional real estate quality photos transformed the website and helped win the trust of potential guests.

Listings with professional photos doubled or tripled the number of bookings and by the end of the month, the entire website revenue had risen by 100%. Sooner afterwards, the company began to focus on entire houses and apartments for rent instead of just rooms.

This shift saw them get their first significant investment, $7.2m in seed funding. Since then, the company has raised a total of $4.4b in funding over 13 rounds.

The 80/20 Software Rule – Building Digital Products in Weeks instead of Months

You're excited! You've identified a pain point or have seen a pressing opportunity that can be harnessed and solved by using software. Perhaps you've even done some early validation with a non-functional MVP (as discussed in Chapter 6 *"What if you don't have the money or skills to build a functioning MVP"*).

But you're also nervous, because now it's time to actually start building the first version of your web application or mobile app.

And, not meaning to scare you, you should be nervous!

Depending on which research you consult, the failure rate of a custom software project is between 50% and 80%. According to four different research firms, only 20% of software projects are finished in a timely manner (and without loss of quality). In fact, research tells us that "the average project runs approximately 200% late, roughly 200% over budget, and contains only two-thirds of the original (agreed upon) functionality."

Don't get us wrong, we're not trying to advise you against building a custom web application or mobile app. Well-designed software can save businesses loads of time and resources.

What we do want, though, is to help you avoid the three-headed monster that seems to gobble up so many custom development projects:

- The development of your app going over budget.

- The project missing your deadline.

- The "finished" app being full of bugs or simply not working as intended (the worst of the three)!

Having run a software development firm for more than 10 years, we've sat across the table from clients who have come to us after spending tens (or even hundreds) of thousands of dollars on custom software development, but are no closer to getting the functionality they've needed in their web application or mobile app.

Outlined in this chapter, we look at why app development projects fail so often and how you can avoid this situation happening with your app. Or maybe you're in this situation right now? In which case, we will outline how you can turn things around as fast as possible!

Why do projects go over budget and miss their deadlines?

Software is complex. Written documents, designs and sketches are easily misinterpreted which means it's very easy for a development team to spend time doing lots of work that doesn't actually benefit the end users of your software (it may even be detrimental to them, which we'll see later)!

If you're paying a software engineer, you want to know that each invoice you pay is resulting in the project getting closer to finishing, right? Unfortunately, in reality, this will only be happening a portion of the time.

Let's say just one developer works on one feature that was misinterpreted (or maybe the feature didn't actually need to be included). This means for at least the hours spent on that feature, you'll be paying for the costs of running a development company (paying programmers, project managers, QA testers, rent and other overheads) without the invoice being directly attributable to you seeing a working app.

For the project to be successful, you'll need the developers to have a complete understanding of the requirements (including the end users), so that they're spending their time incrementally adding value to your software.

Of course 'adding value' sounds great, but how can you tell if that's happened? Hearing, "We're 15% closer", doesn't give you any value, nor does seeing screenshots or hearing promises.

When it comes to writing code, you can't have tangible value without working software that you and your users can log into and use! That's why the key focus for your project, the number one way to avoid overrun budgets and timeframes, is to ask yourself:

"How can I get my hands on a working app as quickly as possible?"

Get to Usable Software as quickly as possible

Around 15 years ago, the FBI had a software project which aimed to digitize all the agency's historic and on-going records. The planned solution was to include a plethora of features, but the cost of development had spiralled to $400 million after four years, and the agency was no closer to its solution.

It was then that Jeff Sutherland took over the project. Sutherland started by asking the question, 'How can we get our hands on working software as quickly as possible?' This led him to radically reduce the scope of the first version of the app and, over the course of a year, by iterating and improving on that initial version, the FBI had a functioning system that cost less than a tenth of the failed project in less than one fourth the time!

Since then, other companies have adopted this 'Agile' or 'Lean' project management approach, which means software can be completed much faster and be working how it was intended to work.

How to simplify down to the first version

How do we figure out what the first version of an app or web application should be? The most effective way to do this is to break everything down into 'user stories'.

What are user stories?

Before you design (or even do rough sketches) you should map out all the ways in which the end users need to use your web application or mobile app.

Instead of talking in terms of 'features' and 'functionality', you should write out basic user stories. These are sequences that users need to go through in order to achieve something useful.

Format: 'As a <user role>, I want <a feature>, so that I can <accomplish something>.'

Example: 'As a sales person, I want a dashboard showing all incoming leads ordered by date, so that these can be handled before doing anything else.'

There will probably be different user roles, and likely numerous user stories for each of those roles, but the great thing about user stories (as opposed to just listing functionality) is that by completing a user story, the development team will have incrementally increased the value of your web application or mobile app.

Each completed user story represents another thing your app can do in the real world. Instead of confirmation from a project manager that 'progress has been made' on the project, you can actually perform the user story yourself.

Once enough user stories have been built by your developers, you'll reach a point where you can release an early MVP version of your app to real customers.

Can you simplify your startup idea?

It can be difficult trimming the fat off your idea. An effective approach to achieving this can be to start writing user stories and prioritise them. Then you can decide what user stories are actually needed for the first version.

By using this method, we've found most clients end up being able to start using the software in the wild after mere weeks of development (instead of months or years).

The 80/20 Software Rule

Hopefully by now you can see the sense in simplifying your software down to a minimal first version. Sometimes, though, it can seem impossible to reduce your web application or mobile app idea down to a simple first version (one that can be built in 1-2 months instead of 9-12 months, or even years).

It's time you heard about our 'Microsoft Word' rule.

You've probably heard of Pareto's 80/20 rule, that just 20% of input (time, resources and effort) produces 80% of your results. The numbers aren't always exact, but the law always seems to come true. It's up to you whether you simply observe it, or whether you harness it to improve your situation exponentially (i.e. stop doing as much of the 80% as you can and do more of the 20% that gets results).

This law applies to software too, and if saving a whole heap of time and money in developing your web application or mobile app sounds good, then you need to take advantage of it!

> "Far more than 50% of functionality in software is rarely or never used. These aren't just marginally valued features; many are no-value features."

– Jim Highsmith, American software engineer and author

In software, we like to call it the 'Microsoft Word rule'. It's highly unlikely that anyone reading this book hasn't used Word and found it useful. However, if you take a look at the standard out-of-the-box tools the software offers, most people only use its core document editing, formatting and possibly collaboration features.

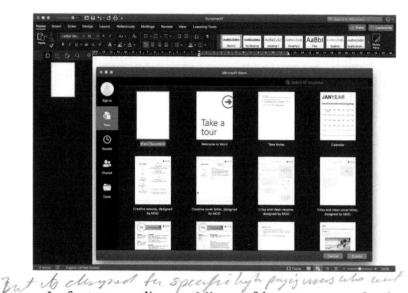

But is designed for specific high paying users who want this feature

In fact, according to Microsoft's own research, the average user uses just 8% of Word's functionality. Think how many millions of dollars worth of software engineering hours were spent by Microsoft in building functionality that their core market simply never uses!

If your company is as big as Microsoft, you can probably afford this kind of wastage. But if you're a startup you'll be shuddering at the thought of having thousands of developer hours spent on functionality that the end user hardly ever (or never) uses.

This is exactly why building less, and launching sooner, is such a better way to approach building your web application or mobile app. You can take your app idea and in 20% of the time have a product that's 80%

finished, which in most cases is all you need for version one (and maybe even all you'll ever need full stop!)

Compare Microsoft Word to OmmWriter, an ultra minimalist document editing software. OmmWriter probably has 1% of the features that Word has, but it captures a large customer base that wants to write in a distraction free environment.

Can simple products be enough of a product to build a business on? Such a product has been pretty lucrative for Barcelona-based Herraiz Soto & Co, the independent creative agency that built OmmWriter. The product has been sold to more than 1 million users.

How to get your MVP built in weeks, not months

There is only so much that can be said in a chapter, but hopefully you've taken away at least one gem that could save your startup thousands of dollars and even months of development!

Let's recap some key points to ensure you avoid the three-headed monster and successfully build a working MVP version of your app:

- **Get your hands on working software as soon as possible, and definitely before 'Version One'** – Learn from the FBI's mistakes. Having a bare bones minimal version of your app that works is 100% better than having a feature-rich enterprise application that is yet to be finished and unusable by you or the end users.

- **User stories are more useful than 'features'** – As each user story gets built, your app becomes more and more useful in the real world. On the other hand, working away at 'features' can mean you've theoretically completed 50% or even 80% of the project and have 0% usefulness (having features built doesn't necessarily equate to usable software that you can test out).

- **Simplify your software project using the 80/20 Principle** – You don't want to build a product like Microsoft Word if your users only ever needed a product like OmmWriter. What are the most important user stories? Rank these in order and choose the 20% of user stories that will produce 80% of the benefits.

Instead of summarising down to three points, if you really want to apply the 80/20 rule, go all the way down to one point, or even a single word – simplify. What would be the simplest implementation of your product idea that would have the biggest impact for your users? Build that first, and iterate from there.

> *"Perfection is achieved, not when there is nothing more to add, but when there is nothing left to take away."*

> – Antoine de Saint-Exupery, Aviator and author

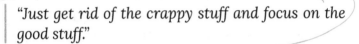

> *"Just get rid of the crappy stuff and focus on the good stuff."*

> – Steve Jobs, Founder of Apple

Start with a simple app, and keep it simple

There are many billion dollar startups that started by creating a very simple product and grew their company by keeping it that way. But this goes against conventional wisdom – shouldn't companies grow and develop their products to be the biggest and best?

In reality, all-in-one, all encompassing software products are mediocre at best, with functionality that mostly works but leaves users with a feeling of mild to high frustration. On the other hand, if you're looking to build a highly profitable company, you want people to love your product, almost irrationally – like 'fanboys' of Apple or Tesla, companies that build simple and user friendly products.

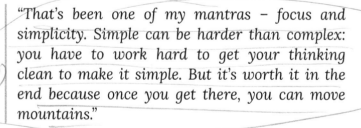

"That's been one of my mantras – focus and simplicity. Simple can be harder than complex: you have to work hard to get your thinking clean to make it simple. But it's worth it in the end because once you get there, you can move mountains."

– Steve Jobs, Founder of Apple

Successful startups that kept their products simple

Canva

Australian-based startup Canva is a graphic design tool which competes with Photoshop. Feature-wise, it offers less than 5% of the functionality that Photoshop does, but that's the main reason it's become so popular.

Marketers that previous used Photoshop (or paid a designer to use Photoshop) can now jump onto Canva and create an attractive, professional graphic in a few minutes using mostly a templatised approach. The product has grown exponentially with its freemium model and is now worth over $1 billion.

Blinkist

Blinkist is an app that summarises bestselling non-fiction books so you can get the key ideas in just 15 minutes – either by text or audio. The app doesn't use any artificial intelligence to produce 'Blinks' (its term for 15 minute summaries), it is driven by a human process of reading and summarising content, and then presenting in the app as a catalog.

Some predicted the idea was too simple to become a fully fledged business, but Blinkist now has around 6 million users and has raised $35 million in funding to date.

Keynotopia

There are lots of software options if you're a UX designer, but Amir Khella found himself skipping the expensive design software that he typically used, and instead used Keynote. He created various UX elements as templates, then copied and pasted them into a new presentation, created hotspots, and essentially built a fully clickable prototype without any dedicated design software.

Surely selling Keynote and PowerPoint templates as a product couldn't be a sustainable business? It turns out it can. Keynotopia has sold its templates to more than 65,000 customers with prices ranging from $97 to $149. It continues to operate today, selling nothing more than Keynote and PowerPoint templates (which are periodically updated to keep in line with current design trends).

Gumroad

Sahil Lavingia launched Gumroad in 2012. Aiming to make the ability to sell online as easy as sharing content on social media, he built the tool without the need for a merchant account, shopping cart or any complicated ecommerce software. You can simply add your Gumroad link to your website, or even a Facebook or Twitter post and you're done.

Despite being such a simple product, Gumroad was able to raise over $8 million in funding and quickly expanded its customer base. The company's direction has changed since then, but its vision has not. Lavingia decided not to shoot for unicorn status or continue down the VC funding route, but he has kept Gumroad running independently and growing profitably (it now has a $4 million annual run rate with less than ten employees).

Large companies that launched products with less features

Whether you want to start and run a successful private company or build the next $1 billion startup, launching with a simple, laser focused product is still a smart way to maximise your chance of success. There are many successful products with countless features that people forget were launched with a focus on simplicity.

For example, Instagram was a very basic social network compared to Facebook. It took the parts of Facebook everyone loved (sharing photos) and removed everything else – no pages, games, posts, apps, events or news articles.

Then there is Google. Now a behemoth with over 85,000 employees, Google started with a very simple website. Compared to search engines such as Yahoo, Lycos and Alta Vista, which had thousands of links and advertisements on their homepages, Google had an almost amateurishly simple homepage and for years didn't have a single advertisement on its search results pages.

While other search engines were trying to become one-stop-shops for everything on the Internet, Google focused on just one thing – search. Ironically, by choosing to go against the grain, Google is now considered the starting page for most people.

Beware of adding features for the sake of features

It's very tempting to continually add features to your product. If you successfully launch a product and receive positive feedback, it can be a knee jerk response to go back and add ten new features. The thing is, even if each of those ten features are useful, they won't necessarily make your product ten times better.

When Joel Gascoigne launched the first version of Buffer, which was limited to Twitter only, it was tempting to quickly add Facebook functionality. Instead he focused on tweaking and improving the Twitter integration and on marketing the tool as it was. The end result was a narrow focused tool that people loved and were happy to pay for, rather than a general purpose tool that was just okay.

> "Beware of the 'everything but the kitchen sink' approach to web app development. Throw in every decent idea that comes along and you'll just wind up with a half-assed version of your product. What you really want to do is build half a product that kicks ass."

– Jason Fried, Founder of Basecamp

The hidden cost of features

Each new feature added to your product makes your software incrementally more complex. The more complex your software, the longer it takes new users to figure out how to use it, and the harder it is for you or your team to support it.

It's a bit like falling into debt or becoming overweight. One or two nice-to-have features won't make much difference but, over time, you'll find your product has become bloated with a multitude of features that now make further development slower and more costly (whenever you write new code, each of the existing features will need re-testing to ensure that you haven't broken anything).

"Innovation is not about saying yes to everything. It's about saying no to all but the most crucial features."

– Steve Jobs, Founder of Apple

Adding every good idea as an additional feature can also hinder your agility in the market. For example, you may want to change your software product in a certain way, but find yourself blocked by certain features previously added that seemed 'a good idea' at the time.

How to add new features without adding bloat

Although you shouldn't add features as soon as your customers ask for them, products will and should evolve over time and you may find certain features just make sense. But how do you choose which features do make sense, and which should be ruled out?

One way to decide is by adding a feature to your user interface, but not actually make it functional. For example, let's say you have a new blogging platform and, as part of the software, you've had requests to include a calendar feature so that authors can plan out future article ideas.

This would be a fairly complex feature, and would definitely add to your support queries. Instead of jumping in and writing code, you could simply add a 'Calendar' link into your app navigation. Users would be able to click on that link, but instead of being taken to the actual calendar functionality, they would see a message saying 'Calendar still in development'. If you have analytics software installed, this will enable you to check the number of people that are clicking on the link and see how many times each user is clicking on it.

Whoops, this feature isn't ready yet! ✖

Document Collaboration is currently in development. You might like to help us build the right solution?

> How do you hope to use document collaboration?

Send Message

You could also add an email opt-in form allowing users to add their email address and indicate that they want to know when the feature is ready. But more usefully, you can also display a text message area with a question: 'Why are you most interested in a Calendar?'. Users can then explain why and how they would use the feature.

Without writing any code, you can gauge user interest and expectations. Perhaps the need is so simple, it would be easier to simply integrate with a third party tool such as Google Calendar. Or maybe the user expectations are so complex, you know for sure you don't want to build it. If that is so, you can look for a dedicated external tool to integrate with, or you may decide that users wanting such complexity fall outside your definition of ideal customer.

Too annoying?

You may think that taking this approach will annoy your users and that might prove to be the case if the feature is critical (e.g. the ability for users to view sent emails in email software might be considered a must-have feature). However, for non-critical features, there are ways to avoid upsetting your users.

When Sheetsu was adding the ability to sync files on Amazon S3, it decided to ship fast by leaving out what some would consider vital functionality (such as the ability to delete a file after it has been synchronised). To avoid annoying users, Sheetsu included a delete link, which whenever a user clicked the link, would automatically open up live chat software with a pre-populated message: 'I need to delete ABC file from XYZ location.' The support team were still able to help the user remove the file (albeit not always right away), while also gathering feedback on the usage of the new functionality and whether it was worth building the full feature set later on.

Start!

Throughout the course of the first half of this book, you've encountered numerous examples of successful MVPs. Small, incomplete products that led to successful companies.

Some of those companies were acquired for millions of dollars, others are now listed on the stock exchange, and others are still running private, profitable businesses.

Some of these founders were software engineers, others were non-technical. Some of the companies started with fully working products as their MVP, others started with nothing more than a video or landing page.

What is common with all, is that they used their current resources to start with some type of product and ship it into the world. That allowed them to test the reaction, get feedback and iterate from there.

"Good enough is good enough. There is time for refinement later. It's not how great you start – it's how great you end up."

– Guy Kawasaki, Investor, Author and early stage Apple Employee

Part 2:
Growth

So You've Built and Launched your App, What Next?

You've done the work, and you've got your MVP. The next most important step for any startup is acquiring customers and scaling your growth. How do you go about that? In Part Two of The 30 Day Startup, we'll provide examples, case studies and stories of how successful startups have managed to acquire or grow their user base.

We also suggest some practical changes that you can implement immediately.

When to read this section of the book?

This part of the book will be most useful when you are in one of the following stages:

- You have just finished your MVP and need to acquire users

- You want to scale your existing business or startup

- You're in need of some inspiration and would like to read about successful growth marketing campaigns

- You want some practical suggestions on how you can promote your product or service straight away

Content Marketing done right

Our definition of Content Marketing is a marketing approach focused on creating and distributing valuable, relevant, and consistent content to attract customer attention and drive desired customer action.

This is just a loose definition – there are exceptions. Not everything you share is your own content – sometimes you share other people's content, just as they too share yours.

Content marketing is important, not just because it works for building trust, generating leads, and cultivating customer loyalty – but also because it has become the new normal to acquire customers' attention.

Some of the main benefits of content marketing:

- Increased visibility of your brand

- Develops lasting relationships with your audience

- Improves brand awareness and recognition

- Creates loyalty and trust, with both your current customers and prospects

- Builds authority and credibility

- Positions your business as an expert in your industry

- Improves lead generation

- Opens channels of communication through social shares and comments

- Helps your customer move through the purchase decision more quickly

- Provides value with no strings attached

There has been a huge surge of content marketing in recent years due to the unique environment of internet, mobile technology, cloud computing, and social media use. This has made it much easier for companies to communicate with their users.

However, content marketing has been around for centuries. Here is an example of successful content marketing from a different time period in history.

Case study

In the late 19th century, Andre and Edouard Michelin faced a major challenge in growing their tyre business. There were fewer than 3,000 cars in France. It was hard to build a tyre company when there just weren't enough cars on the road.

In 1889, the Michelin brothers used content marketing to solve this challenge. To encourage motorists to take more trips – thereby boosting car sales and, in turn, tyre purchases – they produced a small guide handy information for travellers. The guide incorporated handy information such as maps, instructions on how to change a tyre, where to fill up on petrol, and most wonderfully – for the traveller in search of respite from the adventures of the day – a listing of places where they could eat or take shelter for the night.

*image source - https://guide.michelin.com/sg/
history-of-the-michelin-guide-sg

Contrary to popular belief, the Michelin guide wasn't an immediate success. Initially, the brothers handed copies out for free. This practice was brought to a halt by a fateful encounter when Andre Michelin arrived at a tyre shop only to see his beloved guides being used to prop up a workbench. Based on the principle that 'man only truly respects what he pays for', a brand new Michelin Guide was launched in 1920 and sold at seven francs.

The guide expanded to include a list of hotels in Paris and restaurants according to specific categories, while paid-for advertisements were abandoned. The guide also began to award stars for fine dining establishments and published the criteria for starred rankings, which are still highly sought after.

During the 20th Century, the Michelin Guides became best-sellers – more than 30 million copies had been sold worldwide.

The guides enticed drivers to explore more of their country, try different restaurants and stay at unique hotels. The maps helped the drivers get to their desired destinations, while the increased mileage.increased tyre sales. This sort of ingenuity has ensured the company's survival for more than a century when most companies close their doors within five years.

In today's age, companies are no longer limited to printing a physical guide. Brands and companies today can produce blogs, infographics, YouTube videos, e-books, social content, and more. The idea is to make or share information that provides real value to consumers.

- Start making content. Everyone has to start somewhere, so start today. Even Michelin had to start somewhere. Initially the Michelin brothers were not successful, but they honed their guide until it provided real value to their customers.

- Not all content has to be original, you can always write, talk or make a video about other people. The Michelin brothers didn't just write about their company, they wrote about other people's restaurants and hotels.

- Make a list of all the content you need to develop and schedule your content in a calendar. For example, writing or podcasting one story a week. Otherwise it never gets done.

Video Marketing that works

Video Marketing is nothing more then spreading your message or content via video or using video to promote or market your brand, product or service.

Since the advent of super fast broadband and the universal usage of mobile phones, the popularity of videos has skyrocketed.

Marketers have anticipated this trend and started incorporating video into their marketing strategy early on. In the 'results-or-die' situation that many startups find themselves in, a video is a tool that no startup can afford to overlook.

Case Study

Sometimes ignoring everyone and following your gut feeling can work, and in some extreme cases like Squatty Potty, following your bowel can work.

In the startup's video ad named **"This Unicorn changed the way I Poop"**, a prince in funky clothing explains how your bowel works and why Squatty Potty stool is the healthier alternative for your bowel movements. At the same time, a unicorn demonstrates beside him by pooping rainbow-colored soft serve ice cream.

Edwards, the founder of Squatty Potty was initially skeptical of spending a large amount on a video campaign and was concerned the video might be considered crass by the general public. However the risk paid off.

The video received nearly 15 million views the year it released and to date (January 2019) has clocked 40 million+ views in YouTube and 140 million+ views and 1.6 million+ shares on Facebook.

But the biggest win was a revenue growth of 600% for the 2015 year. And most of the new customers found out about the company organically after seeing the online video **"This Unicorn changed the way I Poop"**.

Squatty Potty becoming a smashing viral hit, of course, doesn't guarantee that every funny video will become a viral sensation. In fact, virality is extremely hard to predict. Squatty Potty made multiple videos after the "This Unicorn changed the way I Poop". None of them reached the success at the same level. However, they still get millions of views and video remains a big part of the company's customer acquisition strategy.

Take home message

- Don't wait - just make a video, even if it's just a demo of how to use your startup's product or service.

- Be brave - experiment with various styles in your video, try humor or make it wacky.

- Video will help you get engagement, improve your website's SEO, build your brand, and improve your conversion rate.

Five reasons why your startup's growth strategy should prioritize video

1. Better SEO

Search engines love videos – they see them as high-quality content. Google's algorithms are increasingly prioritizing websites with video content. Having videos in your webpage will automatically increase the rank factor for the 'rich media' content. More content brings with it the opportunity for more keyword labels, including titles, descriptions and tags.

2. More conversions

Videos can make you some serious money. Adding a product video to your landing page can increase conversions by 80%. Wyzowl, an animation video company, found in a 2016 survey that 74% of people were more likely to buy a product if they were able to see it in an explainer video. Another reason why videos are great for conversions is that viewers stay on host websites for longer than they would otherwise . This is especially true for those who aren't big readers (a good rule of thumb is to assume that people's eyes could be tired from looking at a screen all day).

3. Emotional connection and trust

Video content can create a personal connection between the viewer and the brand. Videos enable you to share creativity and really connect with your audience. According to research by Liraz Margalit, a Web Psychologist, campaigns with purely emotional content are twice as effective as campaigns with only rational content. Whether it's a product review, a testimonial or a webinar, having video content will likely grab your audience's attention and keep them wanting more.

4. Catch the consumers eye

Rather than reading extensive copy or filing through online catalogs, video content appeals to even the most dismissive buyers. Consumers can engage, embed, share and comment on video content – all at the touch of a button. Video content is the perfect way to cut the need for reading and easily engage all types of audiences.

5. Easy to share

We often share interesting videos on social media or various messaging platforms as a quick and easy way to get our point across. Moreover, there are copious examples of companies who have managed to successfully utilise video to get viral growth. To reinforce this point, we will now take a look at a couple of case studies and show how you can utilise video to increase engagement, educate or acquire customers for your startup.

What can you implement today?

Making videos used to be hard, but tools like slide.ly and wave.video now make it a lot easier to make videos fast and cheap. These sorts of software have ready-made templates, clips and sounds that you can mix and match to create your own videos.

1. Make one video describing your service or product

2. Make how-to videos in your industry

The Power of Microtools

What are microtools?

This is a strategy that isn't talked about much, but one that can be extremely powerful. In this method, you build a microtool that is useful for your customer. For example, you have just started a new brand for organic, vegan, gluten-free protein powder called "UnicornDust". In this scenario, you could make a microtool which allowed people to come to your website, enter their physical details – such as height, weight, biceps, waist, chest, etc, – and take away a result of how much protein they need in their diet..People could use it without signing up or buying anything from the website.

Tools like these have potential to bring in huge traffic. People often love finding out things about themselves and use these sort of tools online just for fun and/or they share them with their friends.

Moreover, these sort of microtools can be marketed on Producthunt.com and are highly likely to go viral. Here is an example of one such company that has managed to leverage a microtool to its advantage.

Case study - Google's Art and Culture challenge

Google wanted to promote Arts and Culture in the age of 140 characters, 15 second videos and gif memes.

In 2016, Google launched an Arts & Culture app for its online platform through which the public can access high-resolution images of artworks housed in partner museums.

The app brings the museums of the world to your smartphone. Available for free on iOS and Android, it lets users browse more than 70,000 works of art from more than 1,000 museums. Users can read more about the artwork, the artist and the museum, all without having to push through hordes of tourists to get up close.

Google's Arts and Culture institute was founded in 2011, but this was the first time that an app had been launched for such a venture. The institute's objective was to get people interested in Art and Culture. Which is not the easiest of tasks - so how was this problem solved?

The answer is that Google made a microtool and added it to the app. This tool or feature allows you to take a selfie and uses your selfie to find an image in a museum that looks like you.

To give you an example: Here is a selfie of one of the co-authors [Sam] that was taken using Google's Arts & Culture app's microtool.

Inclusion of this selfie feature didn't go unnoticed. Buzzfeed wrote an article about the app titled "Twitter Is Cracking Up Over The Google Arts & Culture Face Match". The piece included photos of the author [Morgan Shanahan], along with humorous results from ordinary people on Twitter. Multiple celebrities jumped on the bandwagon and started sharing their museum look-alikes on social media.

Downloads skyrocketed, reaching 12.8 million over the holiday weekend. By Monday, the app held the coveted #1 spot in both the Android and iOS app stores. Meanwhile, in Paris, 30 Google employees worked through the weekend to keep it up and running, supporting users during peak times of 450,000 selfies per hour.

Key Learnings or Take home message

- Make it about them, not you

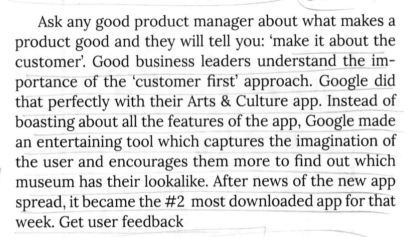

Ask any good product manager about what makes a product good and they will tell you: 'make it about the customer'. Good business leaders understand the importance of the 'customer first' approach. Google did that perfectly with their Arts & Culture app. Instead of boasting about all the features of the app, Google made an entertaining tool which captures the imagination of the user and encourages them more to find out which museum has their lookalike. After news of the new app spread, it became the #2 most downloaded app for that week. Get user feedback

Google Art and Culture web app wasn't successful straightaway. It took the company a few years to develop an app with a selfie feature. Initially, Google Art and Culture mainly existed on a website.

In the app's early days, a couple of developers unveiled an embryonic version at a TED conference. To make the presentation more interesting, they decided to add a 'portrait matcher' feature to compare their own images against Google's database of art.

The audience went crazy over that feature. Google duly took note and went on to build this feature into its app. So the obvious lesson here is to pay attention to your customers' feedback.

- Focus on engagement

Google focused on creating an experience not a transaction. While people are waiting for Google to compare their selfies with paintings in museums, users are building their expectations. They anticipate something funny or elegant in a museum to look like them. Then when the app rewards them with a fun experience, users might start to wonder who friends, partners or spouses look like. Hence, a chain reaction is started.

• PR and Influencers work

No matter how good your product, experience and engagement, if no one knows about your product then no one will use it. The Buzzfeed article kicked things off for the Google Art & Culture selfie app. Then came a wave of TV and Hollywood stars comparing themselves to a painting in a museum and posting on Twitter. Some of the Tweets were hilarious and the millions of people reacted to images of their favorite celebrity's doppelganger.

What you can implement today

- Think of your customer and your industry - what tool can you quickly and cost- effectively make that will either entertain or be useful to your prospective customer.

- If you have no ideas regarding what you should build, ask on Quora or Reddit.

- Contact companies like productdone.com who specialise in making MVPs and microtools. They can cost-effectively build something in six to eight weeks.

Getting traction at Events

What is event marketing?

Event marketing is a strategy that startups use to promote their product or service at an event. The event could be a conference, expo, tradeshow, webinar, seminar or even a meetup.

For example, you have just ran a Kickstarter campaign for your startup that makes party hats for small terriers. And you just made your first 1,000 hats from that funding campaign. Now you are looking at acquiring ongoing customers.

As a next step, you look at all the events that small dog owners attend. And after trolling through the web you find the Annual Handbag Dog Extravaganza. You decide to run an ad campaign on social media using the relevant geo-location, dates, times and hashtags. By also having a physical presence at the event, you can target a large number of potential customers in a short amount of time. You can display posters and banners, hand out pamphlets or merchandise – and, most importantly, get face-to-face feedback from your customers. When you see how customers really use your product, you will know first-hand what customers really like about it.

There are multiple examples of startups that got their initial traction at popular events such as SXSW (an annual conglomerate of film, interactive media, and music festivals and conferences). Here is a case study of one such company.

Case Study - How Twitter got initial traction at SXSW.

In 2007, Twitter was a relatively fresh startup and had limited usage and engagement. Its challenge was to sign up early adopters who would really use the product.

The tipping point for Twitter's popularity was the 2007 South by Southwest Interactive (SXSWi) conference. During the event, Twitter usage increased from 20,000 tweets per day to 60,000. "The Twitter people cleverly placed two 60-inch plasma screens in the conference hallways, exclusively streaming Twitter messages," remarked Newsweek's Steven Levy.

Thousands of people going to SXSW kept tabs on each other via constant tweets. Panelists and speakers mentioned the service, and the bloggers in attendance touted it. Reaction at the conference was highly positive. Blogger Scott Beale reported that Twitter was "absolutely ruling" SXSWi. Social software researcher Danah Boyd said Twitter was "owning" the conference. Twitter staff received the festival's Web Award prize with the remark "we'd like to thank you in 140 characters or less. And we just did!"

Cost to Twitter?

Twitter paid $11,000 to project a visualization of the service on flat-panel screens in the conference hallways. The startup wanted to be seen where there was high foot traffic.

Moreover, Twitter created an event-specific feature that allowed attendees to text a message in order to sign up automatically and follow a handful of 'ambassadors' at SXSW.

End Result

Once Twitter got going at SXSW, it never had to look back. The company experienced rapid growth and had 400,000 tweets posted per quarter in 2007. This grew to 100 million tweets per quarter in 2008. By February 2010, Twitter users were sending 50 million tweets per day!

Key Learnings or Take home message

- Target the right event

Twitter understood its audience. The startup wanted tech savvy, young, early adopters. To achieve this goal, there wasn't a better event than SXSW in 2007.

You must understand the persona of your customer; if you target the wrong event, you end up wasting time, money and resources in the bid to get traction for your startup.

- Capture attention

Twitter caught attention by setting up 60-inch plasma screen TVs to display tweets related to the conference. As the old business mantra goes: you can have the best product in the world, but if no one knows or ever hears about it, then no one will use it.

- Provide value / entertain / make your offering different

Twitter achieved this by showing live data and letting people see the power of this revolutionary product. SXSWers were able to see what people near them were tweeting in real time. Most had never seen anything like this before and so were captivated. They wanted to be in the in-crowd. They wanted to participate. Not only was it a fun experience, they wanted their tweets to appear on screen for others to see.

- Close the deal / sign up

Finally, Twitter created a SXSW-specific feature that allowed people to join Twitter simply by texting 'join sxsw' to its 40404 SMS shortcode. Because most of the attendees were new to their product, Twitter wanted to close the sale (sign up new users) as soon and as effortlessly as possible.

What can you implement today?

- Search and find an event in your industry that your target audience is likely to attend.

- Think of different ways you can capture attention at that event. Offline and online. For example: Facebook ads or Twitter campaign for the hashtag of the event.

- Use a lead capture solution like eventhook.co to capture more higher quality leads at your next event.

Using influencers for promotion

What is influencer marketing?

Influencer marketing is nothing new. The concept involves using someone with social influence to promote your product, service or event. A real life example is getting your wing man to do your pitching.

Or to give you an example in the age of internet, startups and high speed internet, it looks something like this.

You have just finished writing a recipe cook book inspired by Peter Jackson's movie BAD TASTE. How do you promote it in a sea of cook books on Amazon when nobody has heard of you?. One solution is to hire an Instagram influencer to tag food pictures and write about your cookbook's unique recipes. Often, these influencers do not even have to provide a link or talk about a product, they might just have right product placement.

*It is required by law that influencers have to declare any paid promotion as an advertisement to their followers.

In recent years, influencer marketing has gained immense popularity, especially among younger demographics. And influencers can be found in nearly every niche; there is always a guru or an expert making videos on any given topic on YouTube. Moreover, there are blogs, Instagram, podcasts, fan pages and groups on social channels dedicated to following a certain trend or influencer.

The categories that are most disrupted by influencer marketing are gaming, beauty and nutrition industries. In 2017, a New Zealand startup on a shoestring budget took advantage of influencer marketing to generate a huge amount of global traction..

Case Study - *Creating Uproar in the online gaming community*

In 2017, I [Sam] worked as Head of Growth for Uproar.gg Uproar was like air miles for gamers – gamers collect loyalty points for gaming. Uproar sold this engagement to game publishers so they could get early player base established. Uproar's platform also ran tournaments and other competitions for gamers.

- **The challenge**

Gaming space is extremely crowded. Grabbing the attention of gamers is no easy task, especially when hundreds of new games are released every day.

I was given the task of promoting the Uproar platform as a premium place to organise eSports tournaments, build the Uproar brand and build a base for future tournament sponsorships. The allocated budget was a tenth of what an event of this scale would need.

- **Traditional approach**

A traditional approach would be to promote the tournament via online and offline media using ads. The tournament would be organised at a physical location and promoted by spending hundreds of thousands of dollars on marketing, PR and free merchandise.

- **Our approach**

However, we at Uproar took a different approach. Due to logistical challenges of different time zones, Battle Royal games hardly ever run online tournaments that allow gamers from across the world to participate. So we decided to run a PUBG - Battle Royale tournament on a global scale, enabling 100 players (from potentially that many countries) to compete online at the same time.

Allow me to explain how the competition will run.

To raise awareness the tournament, we created an extremely edgy promotional video. To heighten the video's impact, we hired UFC champion Demetrious Johnson to star in it. Not only has Demetrious won multiple championships in his class, but he's also an avid gamer and streamer. It was an absolute pleasure to deal with him

The second influencer we hired was a hacker that we had never met or seen in person. Known by the onscreen moniker of African Rebel Lord, he proved to be unpredictable, charismatic and hilarious – which was exactly what we wanted.

The pair recorded some game play and the result was a provocative and compelling promotional video.

We also got other things right. To make our tournament stick in the memory banks, we gave it a funny name – the 'Golden Chicken' Tournament – and the lucky winner received a gold-plated chicken.

Our event went viral and multiple gaming influencers signed up and started promoting the event on their Twitter and Facebook groups.

- **The result**

Our campaign was massively successful. The promo video received nearly 5 million views on YouTube and 15+ million views on Facebook. We also got tens of thousands of new gamers signing up to the Uproar platform. Perhaps most importantly, we started to get the attention of media companies who wanted to work with us.

The tournament showcased our capabilities and opened doors for us to other businesses in the USA and Europe.

Since I headed this campaign, I have been a huge fan of influencer marketing. Without spending any money on YouTube or Facebook ads, this approach brought Uproar millions of views and helped build its brand in the eyes of its target consumers.

Key Learnings or Take home message

- Social recommendations work. If you like someone and they recommend something then you are much more likely to try it or buy it.

- It is important to find the right influencer for your product or service. Make sure their audience is aligned with your offering.

- Sometimes courage pays off, but sometimes it can backfire. Most startups don't have an established brand name that they need to protect. So while you are still new, you can experiment. Do not be afraid to try something edgy, funny, weird or out of the ordinary.

- Find a way to make your influencers look good. On top of paying them, give them coupons, voucher codes or a free product they can hand out to their fans. You are building their brand as much as they are building yours. Make it a symbiotic relationship.

- No one likes to follow influencers who are always just selling stuff. So talk to your influencers about how they can promote the product without looking like a sell-out. Maybe they can just do an honest review of your product or service, or a tutorial explaining how they use it. Maybe they can organise a competition or some sort of contest for their fans. The possibilities are endless.

What can you implement today?

- Identify the key influencers in your industry that you know you can afford.

- Consult them, understand how they can promote your product without looking like a sell-out to their community.

- Make a deal or let them give out some discount codes for your service or product.

Leveraging Partnership

How to use key partnerships for growth

It can be hard to compete with the giants in any industry. They have endless resources, expertise, experience, existing networks and clientbase. While most startups view their larger counterparts as 'competition', smart entrepreneurs look for established companies in their industry to partner.

As an early stage startup, you need access to existing customer bases. An established company can provide you with that access. However, as companies increase in scale, it becomes harder and more expensive for them to innovate. That's why you should look for a strategic partnership with a larger company. Ideally, the company would share commonalities and target markets, but not be a direct competitor.

For example:

You have just launched your startup that makes self balancing roller blades for 80 year olds. So you might seek to partner with an insurance company or a chain of retirement villages. You could even run a marketing campaign with them.

It makes sense to form this partnership because these companies have an existing customer base that you would like to tap into. In turn, the partnership benefits them because you have a cool new product that can be added to their offerings. This is a fictitious example, but doubtless you get the point. Here is a real life case study of a such a successful partnership.

Case Study - Taxi music

Uber launched in 2009 and since then has partnered with multiple companies and organisations worldwide to speed up customer acquisition, build brand recognition and give the company a point of differentiation. These partnerships include ones with major companies such as Virgin America, Trulia, and Spotify, just to name a few.

However, one of Uber's best known strategic partnerships was formed in 2014, when the company joined hands with Spotify. This means that Uber customers can listen to their own playlists during their ride or choose what they want to listen to from Spotify's streaming catalog.

Essentially, Uber users can connect their Spotify accounts and stream their favorite tunes while riding in an Uber.

Despite multiple clones that launched to take advantage of the ride sharing hype, Uber's partnership with Spotify created a more personal connection with users and this gave it a competitive advantage over rival apps. From a strategic marketing and public relations standpoint, both parties win. Uber and Spotify are both able to increase their audience reach, while raising brand recognition and awareness, and capitalising on the benefits that each brand has to offer.

This Uber-Spotify partnership has been analysed in various blogs and tech news website. You can read in more detail here, or just search Uber Spotify partnership.

* https://qz.com/297658/uber-and-spotifys-deal-is-more-than-just-a-marketing-stunt/

https://brower-group.com/strategic-partnerships-fuel-ubers-road-to-success/

Strategic partnerships are not a new innovation, the concept has been used in the corporate world by established brands for decades. Just as a side note, not all partnerships work out – especially if they don't deliver the desired results. In such instances, it is better to end the partnership early and move on to other marketing technique, or finding a more compatible partner.

Key Learnings or Take home message

- Partnerships can cut customer acquisition costs

The two most important numbers that a VC (Venture Capital) fund wants to know about your startup is the LTV and CAC, i.e. Life Time Value and Customer Acquisition Costs.

Acquiring customers for any new startup can be one of the biggest expenses. One of the easiest ways to reduce your CAC is to form partnerships where you get access to your strategic partners' client base. To form such partnerships, you will have to provide real value to your strategic partners and their existing clients.

- Partnerships can reduce the time taken to acquire customers

'Partnership' is not the only way to acquire customers. You can run Social Media ads or make use of Pay Per Click advertising, or you can write content and have an extensive content marketing plan. However, such strategies can take a lot longer and cost much more. Forming a strategic partnership can be your fast-track to building an initial user base.

- 'Mutually beneficial' can help both brands

You should be looking for non-competitive, adjacent complementary businesses to partner with. Once you're engaged, treat them as your equal. This doesn't mean the partnership will be 100% fair. Ideally, you'll identify a partner who can bring more to the table than you can, with the expectation that they'll demand more to help you grow your company.

While working for a gaming related startup, we would often promote key influencers and twitch streamers on our Facebook page which had more than 100,000 followers. In return, the influencers would review our product or service. This formed a symbiotic relationship that helped everyone.

- A strategic partnership can help you differentiate your product

Numerous smart watches are available today from different brands. Apple's partnership with Hermes has helped its must-have wearable – Apple Watch – rise above a sea of copycat smart watches via a luxury fashion boost.

What can you implement today?

- Think about the needs of your customer, and make a list of other products or services that your customers use.

- Identify other companies that fulfil the needs of your customers but do not directly compete with you.

- If these companies match your brand values, contact them to set up strategic partnerships.

- However, you could start with something as simple as doing a podcast or blog together.

Convert more with exceptional Landing Pages

What are landing pages

A landing page is simply a webpage that serves as an entry point for a website or a particular section of a website. This could be a standalone page on a separate domain name or any page of a website that is optimised to convert more people into customers when they land on it.

A well designed landing page will target a particular audience, such as traffic from an email campaign promoting a free trial of your service or a pay-per-click (PPC) campaign promoting your webinar. You can build landing pages that will allow visitors to download your ebook, whitepapers, webinars, redeem coupons, sign up for free trials, demos etc...

How do they work

Suppose your startup sells pet foods for exotic pets. Your home page will ideally have information about the various types of pet foods that you sell. But suppose you have an Adword campaign for the following keyword phrase, "King Cobra buy pet food". Since this is a unique niche, you would want to make a landing page for this PPC campaign, especially considering King Cobra's favorite snack is other snakes. This way you could customise your landing page to match your niche product. It would be built for conversion. It would have testimonials, product reviews, call-to-action, product description, videos etc.

Such a landing page avoids the pitfall of trying to serve too many consumers at the same time and finding that you cannot serve any of them exceptionally well.

Apart from this fictitious example, one company that has mastered landing page design is Mailchimp.

Case Study

Mailchimp's landing page has all the ingredients necessary to make it a great one.

   −   a clear call-to-action above the fold

   −   the key benefits of using Mailchimp

"You grow with it, and features you didn't know would be useful are ready when you are."

Steven Carse, co-founder, King of Pops

5 Ways to Clear Out Last Year's Inventory

5 tips that will help you turn last year's products into sales.

How to Design a Product Page that Sells

Our tips will help you create an effective product page that grabs the attention of your customers and encourages them to buy your stuff.

19 Tips to Grow Your Business in 2019

We rounded up advice from some of our savviest customers about how to succeed in the new year.

- a testimonial showing user fulfilment

- content that provides real value for free

You'll be in good
company

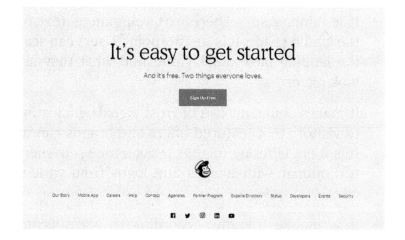

- trust-building 'social proof' that successful companies use Mailchimp

- a strong call-to-action

Key learnings or take home message

Some of the key learnings from Mailchimp's landing page are:

- It has a clean, organized design. A good landing page ensures there is a strong contrast between call-to-action buttons. The bright yellow background makes the darker Sign Up Free button pop out.

- It is minimalistic. There isn't voluminous text on the landing page. It is to-the-point. Users can scan the landing page quickly and find what they are looking for.

- It makes abundant use of trust signals, indicating to visitors that featured offers and brands can be relied on. Offering further reassurance is a 'client testimonial' with images and logos from various clients.

- It is mobile friendly. According to statista.com, more than 52% of web pages browsed on online were via mobiles in 2018.

What can you implement today?

- Make sure your landing page or home page is easy to read, has to-the-point information, a strong call-to-action, and uses social proofs to builds trust, like testimonials and the logos of your client's companies.

Harness the power of FREE

Why give away stuff for free?

Free-Trial and Freemium are well known growth strategies used by startups to acquire first time users. The main differences between Free-trial and Freemium are:

FreeTrial - The software doesn't have a free tier of the product – there is a cost for even the most basic version. However, the software can be tried for a trial period of two weeks to a month. This model is very popular among SaaS products and nearly every SaaS product will give you a free trial period. From Xero to Shopify, hundreds of thousands of SaaS product companies use this type of pricing model.

Freemium - In the freemium model, there is always a free tier of the product. Most of the time it's a very basic version and you will be often offered paid upgrades. This model is very popular in the gaming industry, where they try and sell you cosmetic upgrades via microtransactions or DLC packs – games like Apex Legends, Fortnite, Warframe and Paladins..

Here is a fictional example of how the two packages could be implemented:

You have devised a new fitness trend and started a gym where you combine hot yoga, jiu jitsu and unicycling in one exercise. In the Free Trial version, you would let people use your gym and provide them with all the training as a paying user for the first 15 days. If they wanted to continue beyond that timeframe, they would have to pay full price.

In the Freemium model, access to the gym and exercise program would always be free – but customers could be charged for 'value added services and facilities', e.g: they might have to pay to use the gym showers; Hot Yoga could be cold until they paid extra; Jiu jitsu participants could be charged extra for mats; Unicycle saddles and pedals might need to be purchased each session.

Both these strategies have positives and negatives. According to Rob Walling, "Freemium is like a Samurai sword: unless you're a master at using it, you can cut your arm off."

Neil Patel, the SEO and digital marketing guru, also advises caution: "It's true that many software companies see outstanding results with the free trial business model, but it doesn't imply that everyone should use it. That's just silly. Every single business is different, and the same strategy never fits all.

When it comes to Freemium vs FreeTrial, Canva executed the freemium model extremely well. You can read more about Canva in the case study below.

Case Study - Going from 1K to 10 Million users in 5 years

Canva is a graphic design tool website. I [Sam] have personally used Canva for the last five years and absolutely love it. Canva has the potential to convert anyone with an internet connection into a graphic designer. This quote from Canva's CEO, Melanie Perkins, says it all: "Our goal is to enable the whole world to design."

Canva is simple and very easy to navigate – its interface is user-friendly and intuitive. The user is provided with a wide range of templates, fonts, colors, and free photos to choose from. From Facebook covers to Instagram posts, brochures, infographics, logos, wedding programs, etc – you can design anything and the end result can be amazing.

After Canva made this innovative, easy to use software, it still needed users. And one of the strategies it employed was to let people use Canva for FREE and see for themselves how good it was. They would charge users $1 per stock image or graphic, however they could upload their own images for free.

Moreover, Canva always ensured there was a range of free stock images, graphics and template options. So users generally had an excellent experience and created something in a few minutes that would take an hour to make in Photoshop.

This pricing strategy worked extremely well for Canva. Not only did people love the design tool, they told everyone how much they loved it. As a result, Canva went from thousands of users to millions.

If Canva had put up a paywall after the 14 day trial, I personally would have stopped using it. The only reason I kept using Canva was because the product was completely free. This gave me enough time to get used to it and appreciate it. Over time, I started relying on the design tool more and more. When Canva introduced paid subscriptions, I didn't hesitate because I knew the product well and it had become second nature to use Canva for design work..

Key learnings or take home message

The main takeaway message is for you to enable your customer to use your product, removing any barrier to entry for them.

Free Trials can work if the user needs just a short amount of time to get familiar with your product or service. Conversely, it cannot work if the product is overly complicated and it takes too long to get your head around it. However, Free Trial can be a good option regardless of the size of your target market. That's why Free Trials have become a staple for nearly every SaaS product.

Freemium can work when the product has a huge potential market, tens of millions of users and your product or service has high engagement. Like Fortnite or Canva.

What can you implement today?

- Make sure your users try your product or service for free

- Make sure it's risk free for your users to try your product or service

Implement what you learn

Implementing not just learning is what separates "winners" from unsuccessful people. That is one of the key traits I have observed in successful people.

I have friends who love reading personal development books, but they never translate knowledge into action. I also know entrepreneurs who go to conferences, seminars and training sessions, they take notes, fill out multiple pages. But they never implement anything new. Most of them forget where they kept their notes after a few weeks.

Sometimes going to events, conferences, reading books and learning new things can give us a false sense of security that we are on the right track. However, deeds not words are what ultimately count.

"When William and I wrote this book, we made a point of practising what we preach."

Practising what we preach helped us get to number 1 in Google in just 30 days

We had just started our software development firm, ProductDone.com, where we wanted to specialise in Building Minimum Viable Products (MVPs) and software for non-tech founders.

We wanted to rank number 1 in Google without spending anything on PPC advertising. We thought this goal would take months, if not years, to achieve. But in reality it took just 30 days.

In January 2019, we began by focusing on our customers' needs. We asked ourselves: what do our customers want, what is the most common question they ask us, and how can we solve their problems and answer their questions without asking anything in return?

The insight gained from this process led us to build our first microtool - BuildMyMVP.com

We have already introduced the concept of microtool in an earlier chapter (see page 89) when we told the story of how Google used a microtool to promote their Art and Culture app.

What is BuildMyMVP?

BuildMyMVP is a web based microtool. This tool gives users the ability to quickly find out how much their MVP would cost to develop and how long it will take. It is really easy to use, requires no credit card or login to use, and takes just a minute to use.

In the first version of BuildMyMVP, users choose various options about what they want in their MVP and end up with a summary of the features their MVP will have, approximate cost, and time it will take to build.

In an ideal world, we would want our software or tool to actually build an MVP for users. However, developing a software tool like this would take us months. Plus we wanted to stay true to our message and build something within 30 days, so we released the first version with limited capability.

Here is a screenshot of www.buildmymvp.com ver 1.0

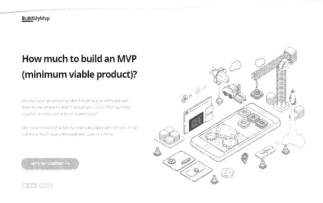

Users click on the "Let's get started" button and are posed a series of questions based on our algorithm.

These questions might differ based on user choices and their specific requirements. At the end of this short process, they will receive a cost and time summary to guide them going forward.

In the Version 1.2 of BuildMyMVP, we want to provide an option for people to build an MVP themselves if they have a zero dollar development budget! So in this version, users will be provided with templates and guidance for free so they can do it all themselves. Our idea is to provide value to users.

The Result

In the first few days of launching BuildMyMVP, we didn't receive much traffic. However, we started sharing our microtool in places like Producthunt, Indihackers, betapage, reddit, Hackernews, Linkedin, Facebook groups, etc. And within a month, it had built enough "ground sell" for us to start receiving organic traffic.

- Here is a breakdown of the numbers:

- Week 1 new sessions: 160

- Week 1 new leads: 2

- Month 1 new sessions: 10,000

- Month 1 new leads: 80

- No.1 on Google globally for search term, "Build my MVP"

- No.8 in search for generic search term, "Build an MVP"

- "Build", "my" and "MVP" are all generic keywords and do not contain a brand name

We think BuildMyMVP was successful because it solved a real problem and met a real need. Most people contact us because they have two main questions: how much will it cost to build and how long will it take?

We answered these questions without requiring people to signup or enter their email address to use our product. This made it user friendly and so people wanted to share its benefits. Nearly 30% of visits in the first two months to our product were from social media and people sharing about our tool.

Finally, a web tool or a micro tool is more than just a blog or piece of content. There is nothing wrong with writing content, but since there are no barriers to entry, anyone can do it. That's why there are probably 3 billion blog posts out there. And it has become extremely hard to stand out from the noise. Doing something challenging has its advantages – and one of those advantages is that it is harder for your competitors to copy.

How you can start building your own micro tool today

Step 1: Find a problem that your potential customer is trying to solve.

Example - If you are a lawyer, then think about what is the most common question that people ask you or your receptionist.

Maybe they want to know how much a lawyer will charge.

If you are a Venture Capitalist, then think of why do most entrepreneurs contact you.

Maybe they contact you because they want to know if they are eligible for funding.

Step 2: Find a simple easy way to solve it.

In the lawyer example, make a web-based tool that allows prospective clients to enter their problem and find out instantly how much it would cost to solve their problem. Similarly, the Venture Capitalist's tool will help founders find out if they are eligible to get funding by using this web-based tool.

Step 3: Can you automate the process? And provide the service for free?

It is best if the tool can run on its own without requiring human intervention. This will reduce your costs and you can potentially provide it for free to people to use.

Step 4: Can you make it fun and easy?

The microtool should not be cumbersome to use; it should not require a complex sign up and boring interface.

Step 5: Build a tool from your learnings from step 1 to step 5.

(If you do not have software development experience, find a company that has a history of delivering results for its clients.)

Step 6: Share your tool to your own networks and get feedback.

Step 7: Improve your tool, fix any bugs.

Step 8: Share it in various directories, forums, and aggregator websites, such as: Producthunt, Indihackers, betapage, reddit, Hackernews, Linkedin, Facebook groups, etc.

Step 9: Improve your tool as you learn how people use it and from other feedback you receive.

Step 10: Release version 2.0, and repeat from Step 6.

Finally, if you are stuck, please feel free to reach out to me Sam Kamani, on Linkedin. I often advise or mentor startups in my spare time.

Funding

Outside Funding for your Startup: How, Why and Why Not?

Creating and growing a startup requires agility and getting your product in front of as many potential users as possible. That's why startups try to get investors as early as possible.

If there are two startups with a product solving the same problem, the one with $10 million in funding is going to have to scale Mount Everest in order to beat the startup with $250 million.

One of the most successful startups in recent times is Amazon. In 1994, Jeff Bezos started the company with a long-term business strategy, which simply wouldn't have been possible without venture capital.

For 20 years straight, Amazon made negative profits in order to gain market share. But playing the long game eventually paid off – in 2018 it become one of just two companies in history to have a market cap of more than $1 trillion.

That said, finding investors is not the only route for startups. Plenty of bootstrapped companies never took a cent in investment in their early years, which allowed their founders to retain the majority, if not all, of the equity and have complete control of their destiny.

Bootstrapped Startups

Retaining control is the main reason you should consider bootstrapping your startup, at least for as long as possible. Venture capitalists are playing a game, they invest in ten startups with the hope that one of those companies will become a Unicorn and earn them a 50x, 100x or more return.

What if the other nine companies don't knock it out of the park, but still manage to grow to respectable $25 million per year businesses? That equals a failure in the eyes of investors who would like to see the company sold or liquidated, so their remaining investment can be put to work at the next potential Unicorn startup.

> "I think that venture capital money kills more businesses than it helps. Lots of businesses could be great $10 million, $20 million businesses, but they're not allowed to be. [They've] got to be $200 million or $500 million or a billion."
>
> – Jason Fried, Founder of Basecamp

Basecamp

Basecamp is an online project management tool which was launched by Jason Fried and David Heinemeier Hansson in 2004. The founders are famous for their outspoken anti-Silicon Valley stance, especially when it comes to funding and growth. They have turned down investment offers from hundreds of venture capitalists and private equity firms.

Although the pair did take an undisclosed private investment from Jeff Bezos in 2006, Basecamp has remained profitable year on year solely from its product subscriptions. Today, annual revenue is estimated to be as high as $168 million.

MailChimp

When Ben Chestnut and Dan Kurzius started MailChimp, an email marketing service, they were entering a market full of VC-backed competitors with deep pockets. After early success, they met with potential funding partners, but decided to go down the road less traveled and maintain full control of their company.

MailChimp now has an estimated annual run rate close to $500 million and has become the defacto email marketing service.

"If you want to run a successful tech company, you don't have to follow the path of 'Silicon Valley'. You can simply start a business, run it to serve your customers, and forget about outside investors and growth at any cost."

– Ben Chestnut, Co-founder of MailChimp

Atlassian

When Mike Cannon-Brookes and Scott Farquhar founded Atlassian in 2002, they funded the startup by racking up a relatively minor $10,000 in credit card debt. From there, they focused on a profit-led growth strategy for eight years until they finally raised $60 million in funding in 2010. Because they had bootstrapped the company previously, they were fully in the driver's seat when they agreed those funding terms.

Unicorns (startups worth over $1 billion) typically go through multiple rounds of funds, which means the founders will often only own around 10% of the company. In Atlassian's case, Cannon-Brookes and Farquhar still owned an astounding 74% of the company when it went public in 2015. It now has a market cap of over $22 billion.

Type of funding and different stages of funding Startups

- Pre-seed funding

Pre-seed funding is the earliest form of funding. Often this is used to finance the ideation stage. The money to fund a pre-seed stage typically comes from the founders themselves, their families, friends and family, and maybe an angel investor or an incubator. This sort of funding is generally under $250,000. Sometimes as little as $10,000.

- Seed Funding

Seed funding, sometimes also known as seed money or seed capital, is a form of funding in which an investor invests capital in a startup company in exchange for an equity stake in the company. The name explains it all, sometimes the seed grows into something and the startup goes on further to Series A and beyond. Otherwise, the startup might decide to discontinue its offering and fold. Seed funding ranges mostly between $500,000 and $2 million. However, it may differ from country to country.

- Venture capital and series A,B, C, D... funding

Once a startup makes it through the seed stage and has gained some kind of traction – whether evidenced by numbers of users or views, revenue or other key performance indicator (KPI) – and the fledgling company is ready to raise a Series A round to lift it to the next level.

According to CB Insights, 46% of companies carry on to raise a Series A after seed funding round.

Depending on the startup and the ecosystem that the money is being raised in, the amount of funding raised in Series A can vary to a huge degree.

If the startup continues to grow, it will go on to more rounds of funding to enable further expansion or it will be acquired by another larger company.

- Crowdfunding

Crowdfunding is the method of raising money through the collective efforts of friends, family and individual investors. One of the best known crowdfunding platforms is Kickstarter. Entrepreneurs generally use this platform for fundraising when they just have a prototype and want to scale production, or when they want to get the word out to early adopters.

There are three main types of crowdfunding:

- Donation-based crowdfunding, where you ask your audience to support your product or service because it has a strong social benefit. .

- Rewards-based crowdfunding, where those who invest in your startup get first access to your product or service.

- Equity-based crowdfunding, where those who support you get an equity stake in your company.

- Business loans

A business loan available to an entrepreneur will vary depending on the location of the startup and entrepreneur. However, most banks and some private finance companies offer business loans to startups. This is one

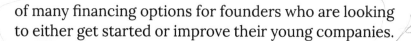

of many financing options for founders who are looking to either get started or improve their young companies.

- Private business grants

Multiple government organizations provide grants for new tech startups.

In the USA, these grants come in three different forms: federal, state and local. In some smaller countries like New Zealand, there are special government-funded organizations – like Callahan Innovation, ATEED, Regional Partners and more – who provide grants to start-ups. Each country has its own version of similar organizations that support startups with grants and funding.

When is the right time to go for funding?

People often think the formula for launching an Internet startup is as simple as coming up with a great idea and then securing funding to go and build the app or software. In reality, unless your name is Jack Dorsey or Elon Musk, investors will never open their checkbook for an idea by itself.

The case studies in this book highlight examples of founders who have first built an MVP for their idea, and then gained validation as evidence that their app or software product can succeed. It was only after they demonstrated traction that they were able to get funding for their idea.

Funding starts after you launch your MVP

In chapter 6, we outlined a number of ways to build an MVP for your product. Depending on your idea, any one of these methods (a fully functional MVP, a Concierge MVP, a Wizard of OZ MVP or a Landing page MVP) can be enough to create the initial buzz needed to impress potential investors and help you get funding to build the full product.

"Most people think it's all about the idea. It's not. Everyone has ideas. The hard part is doing the homework to know if the idea could work in an industry, and then doing the preparation to be able to execute on the idea."

– Mark Cuban, Entrepreneur and Investor

Next Steps?

Right, now you have an idea. In the real world, ideas are worthless; in order to make them valuable, you need to execute.

Some people compare trying to build a successful tech startup to spending your money on lottery tickets. Actually, your chances of success will be much higher than that.

In the consumer market, there are close to 3 billion smartphone users who can download your app. And while it sounds like an impossible feat to carve out a market from that user base, remember that it wasn't so long ago that Facebook was seen as invincible. Now the social network is on shaky ground and only hanging on because of its foresight in acquiring Instagram and Whatsapp.

Then there are the millions of companies who are still using outdated Excel spreadsheets and therefore represent a huge potential market for a secure, cloud-based, software-as-a-service product. In fact, targeting the B2B market reduces your risk substantially as your product simply needs to provide value that outweighs the cost.

Does that mean there's no risk in creating a tech startup? No, in business there is always risk, but with risk comes rewards.

Start now by deciding what your Minimum Viable Product can be and thinking how you can push it in front of the right people.

If you don't have the skills to build the product yourself, you can use an online calculator like www.BuildMyMVP.com to find out how much it can cost to get your MVP built by an agency.

Still need more help? Want to show us your MVP? Drop us a line and we'd love to chat!

Sam Kamani
sam@productdone.com

Will Schmidt
will@orchid.co.nz

Endnotes

References

What Multi Billion Dollar Industry will be Created because of Your Startup?

- Instagram photo sharing app was acquired
  https://techcrunch.com/2012/04/09/
  facebook-to-acquire-instagram-for-1-billion/

- Facebook acquired the messaging app WhatsApp
  https://www.forbes.com/sites/parmyolson/2014/10/06/facebook-closes-19-billion-whatsapp-deal/#387f27435c66

- ...earn upwards of $1m for a single Instagram post
  https://www.cnbc.com/2018/07/31/kylie-jenner-makes-1-million-per-paid-instagram-post-hopper-hq-says.html

- In New Zealand, a business school graduate
  https://www.nzherald.co.nz/business/news/article.cfm?c_id=3&objectid=11733446

- According to Jessie Hagen of U.S. Bank
  https://twitter.com/TozzaPlus/status/983229842501009409

- In 2011, Eric Ries wrote the book
  Ries, E. (2011). The lean startup: How today's entrepreneurs use continuous innovation to create radically successful businesses. New York: Crown Business.

- "In big companies...many months are spent...
  https://basecamp.com/books/Getting%20Real.pdf
  Page 11

Airbnb: How Less than 5 Users Validated Starting a $30b Company

- A key turning point for Airbnb was when they hired a professional camera

  https://ajharringtonphotos.com/2017/07/25/how-professional-photos-helped-make-airbnb-a-success/

The 80/20 Software Rule – Building Digital Products In Weeks Instead of Months

- Depending on which research you refer to....
  Dorsey, Dr P. (2005). Top 10 Reasons Why Systems Projects Fail. Retrieved from: www.ksg.harvard.edu/m-rcbg/ethiopia/Publications/Top%2010%20Reasons%20Why%20Systems%20Projects%20Fail.pdf

- "the average project runs approximately 200% late..."
  SCL. (2013, November 4). Software Development: How the Traditional Contract Model Increases the Risk of Failure. Retrieved from www.scl.org/site.aspx?i=ed31869

- Far more than 50% of functionality...
  Jim Highsmith. (2012). Build Less, Start Sooner. Retrieved from http://jimhighsmith.com

- According to Microsoft's own research

All About Agile. (2012). Retrieved from http://www.allaboutagile.com/ agile-principle-8-enough-is-enough/

Start with a simple app, and keep it simple

- When Sheetsu were adding the ability https://blog.sheetsu.com/ mvping-features-with-intercom-f33c5a5d290b

- "Good enough is good enough..." The Art of the Start 2.0 by Guy Kawasaki

Content Marketing done right

– Contrary to popular belief the Michelin guide...

https://guide.michelin.com/sg/history-of-the-mi-chelin-guide-sg

– During the 20th Century

https://guide.michelin.com/sg/ history-of-the-michelin-guide-sg

Video Marketing that works

– They received nearly 15 million...

https://www.adweek.com/brand-marketing/ squatty-pottys-ceo-ignored-everyone-made-in-sane-video-and-boosted-sales-600-168526/

– But the biggest win was that their revenue grew 600% this year...

https://www.adweek.com/brand-marketing/
squatty-pottys-ceo-ignored-everyone-made-in-
sane-video-and-boosted-sales-600-168526/

— Having videos in your webpage...

https://www.lemonlight.com/blog/
how-will-video-help-seo-ranking/

— In the app's early days...

https://www.bloomberg.com/news/arti-
cles/2018-01-22/google-figures-out-how-to-
make-people-care-about-art-selfies

Power of Microtools

— Downloads skyrocketed, reaching 12.8 million...

http://www.econtentmag.com/Articles/Editorial/
Industry-Insights/What-Marketers-Can-Learn-
from-Googles-Arts-and-Culture-App-123446.htm

Getting traction at Events

— The tipping point for Twitter's popularity...

https://en.wikipedia.org/wiki/
South_by_Southwest

— Twitter paid $11,000 to put a visualization of the
service

https://mashable.com/2011/03/05/
sxsw-launches/#JMg1FyFLd5q8

— Twitter users were sending 50 million tweets per
day.

https://www.telegraph.co.uk/technology/twitter/7297541/Twitter-users-send-50-million-tweets-per-day.html

- Finally Twitter created a SXSW-specific feature ...

https://techcrunch.com/2011/01/04/twitter-foursquare-sxsw/

Using influencers for promotion

- It is required by law...

https://www.bbc.com/news/technology-46960179

Leveraging Partnership

- Uber has partnered with several...

https://brower-group.com/strategic-partnerships-fuel-ubers-road-to-success/

- However one of their most well known...

https://www.businessinsider.com.au/uber-partners-with-spotify-to-personalize-music-in-rides-2014-11?r=US&IR=T

Convert more with exceptional landing pages

- Their page is mobile friendly. According to statista. com...

https://www.statista.com/statistics/241462/global-mobile-phone-website-traffic-share/

Harness the power of FREE

- Quote on Freemium retrieved from https://www.appcues.com/blog/free-trial-vs-freemium , blog post written by Wes Bush

- Quote on FreeTrial from https://neilpatel.com/blog/free-trial-might-be-dangerous/, blog post written by Neil Patel

- Quote on Canva take from https://blog.mark-growth.com/growth-story-how-canva-acquired-10-million-users-within-5-years-bfe5275b321c,

Funding

- "I think that venture capital money kills more businesses..."

  https://www.recode.net/2019/1/23/18193685/venture-capital-money-kills-business-base-camp-ceo-jason-fried

- ...turned down investment offers from hundreds of venture capitalists...

  https://www.forbes.com/companies/basecamp/#7daaeccc47b7

- ...annual revenue is estimated to be as high as $168 million

  https://medium.com/@hungrycharles/basecamp-the-small-bootstrapped-multi-billion-dollar-company-9573988a1435

- When Ben Chestnut and Dan Kurzius started MailChimp

https://www.nytimes.com/2016/10/06/technology/mailchimp-and-the-un-silicon-valley-way-to-make-it-as-a-start-up.html

- When Mike Cannon-Brookes and Scott Farquhar founded Atlassian

  https://www.inc.com/jeremy-quittner/atlassian-ipo-one-of-bigggest-in-2015-profitability-is-key.html

- ...founders will often only own around 10% of the company

  https://www.quora.com/How-much-equi-ty-do-unicorns-founders-typically-have

- According to CB insights...

  https://www.cbinsights.com/research/venture-capital-funnel-2/

Disclosure

We have worked with the following companies named in this book either as a consultant, advisor or director. We have a relationship or equity interest with them either presently or at some point in the past.

- ProductDone

- Orchid

- Uproar

- Better Web

- FreightLegend

- EventHook

We also have equity and relationship interests in many more companies beyond those listed above.

Acknowledgements

We owe a tremendous debt of gratitude to the many people who have helped make this book a reality. A big thank you to all the entrepreneurs for trying, failing and getting back up to stay in the game. Reading other people's stories gave us courage to write our first book.

Also, we would like to thank the team members of Orchid and ProductDone for all their help and encouragement in writing this book.

About the Authors

Sam Kamani

Sam is co-founder and CEO of ProductDone, the company on a mission to democratize software development. Since graduating in Computer Science, Sam has worked in three continents and before starting ProductDone was working with startups in New Zealand and Silicon Valley. A serial entrepreneur and frequent speaker at business events, Sam has advised both startups and established businesses in innovation and growth strategy.

Will Schmidt

Will is the head honcho at Orchid, a software development shop based in Auckland, New Zealand, that combines innovation and business strategy to help startups and corporates build exciting digital products. Orchid also designs and builds its own niche software-as-a-service products in various industries.